Metallica

The Early Years And The Rise Of Metal

by Neil Daniels

Independent Music Press

DEDICATED TO

CLIFF BURTON
(1962-1986)
&
RONNIE JAMES DIO
(1942-2010)

CONTENTS

Hetfield

© photo courtesy of Brian Rademacher/Rockeyez

Ulrich

© photo courtesy of Andre Csillag/Rex Features

Hammett
© photo courtesy of Brian Rademacher/Rockeyez

Newsted
© photo courtesy of Brian Rademacher/Rockeyez

Burton
© photo courtesy of Richard Galbraith

Part I

The Early Years

Brian Tatler of Diamond Head
© photo courtesy of John Tucker

Foreword by Brian Tatler of Diamond Head

It's fairly well documented that a seventeen-year-old Danish lad named Lars Ulrich had bought our debut album in 1980 from a mail order advert in *Sounds* music mag and had written several times to our fan club. He then made the pilgrimage from Los Angeles to the UK to see Diamond Head perform at the Woolwich Odeon on Friday, July 10, 1981. After the show he made his way backstage and introduced himself; we all took to him and he ended up staying with Sean and I at our parents' houses for around five weeks, immersing himself in the world of Diamond Head. Then when Lars went back to the US he formed a band with a guitarist he knew named James Hetfield.

Around January, 1982, Lars wrote me a letter explaining that he had persuaded "this geezer in LA" (Brian Slagel of Metal Blade) to put a track called 'Hit The Lights' by his band Metallica on a compilation of ten new, young LA metal bands. I was busy with Diamond Head and so this piece of momentous news went in one ear and out the other. Nonetheless I wished him good luck.

My next encounter was to be when Metallica released their 'Creeping Death' 12" vinyl EP in November, 1984, on the Music For Nations label. I was sent a copy because on the B-side was a cover of Diamond Head's 'Am I Evil?'; our singer Sean Harris and I listened carefully to the record and were flattered that a band had covered one of our tunes on record, it was a curious feeling but of course we knew it was just Lars (the big Diamond Head fan) on an indie label so neither of us had any idea about the potential of Metallica or how important they would become. We did not even have a clue as to how important this recording would be to the future of Diamond Head and how much money it would eventually make for us.

The first time I actually met the rest of the band was September 20, 1986 when Metallica were appearing at the Birmingham Odeon in support of their groundbreaking LP, *Master Of Puppets*. Lars had called me on the day of the show and invited me along. Once I had picked up my pass and found my way backstage, Lars introduced me to James Hetfield, Kirk Hammett and Cliff Burton. I had thought Metallica were still a small/cult metal band but I was very surprised to see around 1800 rabid fans packed into the venue, especially as this was their first UK tour and their first time in Birmingham. It had taken Diamond Head years to achieve this same sort of following in our home town! There was definitely something happening here, Metallica were going to be the next big thing. I was invited up onstage with them to play 'Am I Evil?' and it was a moment I will never forget, not many people can claim to have played onstage with that line-up of Metallica.

Lars Ulrich is the only person I have ever met who started out as a metal fan and ended up in the biggest band in the world, a truly awesome achievement and I can honestly say that all the success has not changed him; he is still the huge metal fan, full of enthusiasm for what he does, and goes out of his way to make people feel comfortable and welcome. I am very proud of the contribution I have made to their incredible journey.

Brian Tatler
September, 2011
www.diamond-head.net

Introduction

"Our first four albums were very Euro metal."
Kirk Hammett [i]

"Well, Cliff Burnstein who signed us to our new management deal in the States has this big belief that what we are doing will be the next big thing in heavy metal, especially in the States which is something like 80% of the market, and this whole Ratt, Mötley Crüe, Quiet Riot, Black 'N Blue thing will get kinda old and die out and that Metallica will lead the way in a sort of new true metal trend." So said Lars Ulrich in 1984. "One step further than say Iron Maiden who are at the moment the most extreme metal band with major success."[ii] Those words would prove rather prophetic...

Metallica literally changed the face of metal. They didn't do it with one album, of course; they did so over a period of time. They built up a fanbase and conquered the metal world almost single-handedly. They had a passion for metal; it wasn't about the scene, or the money or even the booze and women – it was all about the music. It was about metal. Signing to Q-Prime management company was followed by their elevation to being megastars but their foundations were based on a DIY approach inspired by the New Wave Of British Heavy Metal bands, in particular Diamond Head; a gruff working-class band from Stourbridge in the English Midlands.

Those first four albums by Metallica remain cornerstones in heavy metal. While the final record of that quartet *...And Justice For All* still causes contention within the Metallica fanbase, there's no doubt that the early years of Metallica from 1981 to 1989 laid down the foundations for the birth of American metal. Metallica were literally the bridge between the British heavy metal bands of the late 1970s and the American bands of the 1980s. Metallica also spearheaded the famed Bay Area thrash scene and led the Big Four of the thrash bands, with the remaining three being Megadeth, Slayer and Anthrax. The holiest of the unholy of American thrash.

Some naïvely and erroneously believed that Metallica were just a flash in the pan with limited appeal – boy did they prove everyone wrong! This book is chiefly about the origins of the band, the music that inspired them and their first four albums. Regardless what fans think of the production of *...And Justice For All,* it is still a vital album in the band's mighty arsenal and the last Metallica album of the 1980s. Of course, we all know they began the following decade as an almost entirely different sort of band; they sounded different and looked different. Their roots, however, are firmly cemented in thrash metal. This book will endeavour to show how fundamental those first four albums are, not only in Metallica's back catalogue but also the metal genre as a whole. It seemed as though once Metallica and their ilk began to spread the metal disease around the world, British metal was left in the past. Long gone were the days of bands like Sabbath and Purple. The rise of American metal had begun!

This is not the only book written on Metallica; there is a whole library of books that in various ways catalogue and chart the enduring legacy and music of the band but this is the only book to specifically detail the most important era of their history. When it all started and where it all began. When fans refer to Metallica's music they often refer to those first four albums; certainly anything after their fifth album *Metallica* (aka *The Black Album*) is sometimes talked about with mixed opinion. The reason why this book stops after *...And Justice For All* is because *The Black Album* (1991) changed the sound of the band, quite literally. It can be argued that they ceased being a thrash band and adopted a more commercial metal sound; there was a big leap. A very big leap. The aforementioned 1991 album was the bridge between early day Metallica and latterday Metallica. Had Metallica compromised their sound? There is a definite divide in the band's career and many fans tend to side with the earlier stuff. Some even discount ...*And Justice For All* and thus pin-point the first three albums – *Kill 'Em All*, *Ride The Lightning* and *Master Of Puppets* – as the band's most significant work but this author personally feels the fourth album (despite its production and the over-long songs) also warrants inclusion in a book dedicated to the early years of the band.

This is not a biography of the band; it's the story behind the early years of Metallica and the music that inspired them. It's a study of their first albums and a chronology of events between 1981 and 1989, and deliberately takes a different angle from other works in the field (the best of which are undoubtedly Joel McIver's now classic bio of the band *Justice For All* and his Cliff Burton tome *To Live Is To Die*; and also Mick Wall's recent masterly biography *Enter Night*; not forgetting Ross Halfin's fantastic pictorial book *Ultimate Metallica)*.

Metallica created their best work in this era: is it any wonder that *Ride The Lightning* and *Master Of Puppets* constantly come up in various polls of classic albums or great riffs both within and outside the metal genre? Those albums along with their debut *Kill 'Em All* and their fourth opus ...*And Justice For All* have stood the test of time and hold up alarmingly well in the 21st Century when metal has become in many respects a lot more technical. There is almost a naïvete about those first four Metallica albums but also an honesty, a rawness and large doses of aggression which are now lost in time. Metallica is a different type of band these days and they could never replicate what they created during that era; if they wanted to they would have probably done it by now, anyway. Those albums were as much about youth as anything else.

The thirst for all things Metallica has yet to be quenched. There is an endless interest in the band. As well as telling the story of the band between the years 1981 and 1989, this book also contains a chronology of the albums that came after ...*And Justice For All* and a series of potted histories on some of the most important American thrash metal bands of the era. Whatever people might think of Metallica in the 21st Century, there's no doubting the earlier brilliance of the band.

METALLICA

1981 to 1989 was the period in which Metallica were outlaw metal musicians with a don't-give-a-fuck attitude that literally promised them not only cult status but crowned them kings of the underground American metal scene; of course, they became bigger than that. Much bigger. Subsequent decades saw them attacked and criticised by outsiders as well as their own fanbase for 'betraying' their metal roots but in the beginning they were adored; they were unique and innovative. Metallica knew what metal fans wanted; what they craved. It was all about full-throttle riffs, aggressive vocals, pounding drums and a kick-arse bass. It was thrash fuckin' metal, American style. All hail!

Neil Daniels
November, 2011
www.neildaniels.com

The Birth of the Monster

1981-1982

"I trace most of what's going on today back to 1976 in England, when the punk movement started. Most of today's metal scene is inspired by that – when all the bands in England said, 'Fuck the excess, fuck the grandeur.' It was brought back to a minimalist approach of people wanting to do their own records, not caring about sellable images."

Lars Ulrich[iii]

On June 22, 2010, Metallica, Megadeth, Slayer and Anthrax – otherwise known in metal circles as the Big Four – performed on the same bill at the Vasil Levski National Stadium in Sofia, Bulgaria. The concert was part of an event where the Big Four would, for the first time, tour together as part of the popular Sonisphere Festival. The Bulgaria show was the third in a succession of seven such events but what made it especially popular was that it was transmitted live via satellite to 800 cinemas worldwide (and later released on DVD). It also provided a mouth-watering moment for metal fans as every member of the Big Four (bar Tom Araya, Kerry King and Jeff Hanneman of Slayer) came together onstage for an historic version of Diamond Head's absolute classic NWOBHM track 'Am I Evil?'. Lars Ulrich explained to *Revolver* magazine: "The reason we picked 'Am I Evil?' is because obviously playing a Metallica song would've seemed a little selfish. All of the musicians would certainly share that thread in Diamond Head in terms of influence. It's probably difficult to find a band that's more responsible for, or at least indirectly responsible, for thrash metal. And 'Am I Evil?' is just a great, anthem-like song that also has the quality of not being super-complicated … it just seemed like a logical choice."[iv]

The Big Four popularised thrash metal in the 1980s although

there would be discontent and some ill-feelings between various members for quite some time. Nevertheless, what the event did show is that thrash metal is as popular now as ever before. It was a world away from Metallica's underground beginnings...

The monster was actually born in LA at the tail-end of 1981 although notably they developed and enhanced their sound in San Francisco, once the cultural hub of the late 1960s hippie movement where the likes of Jefferson Airplane, Santana and Grateful Dead reigned supreme. As also noted, aspiring drummer Lars Ulrich was a keen enthusiast of British heavy metal and hard rock, particularly the movement known as the New Wave Of British Heavy Metal, more popularly dubbed NWOBHM.

Between 1979 and 1981 aspiring rockers formed bands literally all over the UK. Not confined simply to the popular cities such as London and Birmingham, these bands also came from as far afield as Sheffield, Newcastle and Manchester. They took a basic DIY approach to their music; much of it was self-released though some bands did attract the notice of London record labels. The big league NWOBHM players included Iron Maiden, Def Leppard, Saxon, Diamond Head, Tygers Of Pan Tang, Girlschool and Venom while lesser known names such as Blitzkrieg, Samson, Sweet Savage and Demon also spring to mind though there were many, many more bands from that era. Most of them, however, have faded into the annals of metal history.

The interesting thing about the NWOBHM bands is that there was more to their music than just good old electric riffs; some bands like Paul Di'Anno-era Iron Maiden were inspired by punk music as much as heavy metal and hard rock. The sounds of Birmingham metal band Black Sabbath – the pioneers of the genre – and London hard rockers UFO can be heard in their music; Maiden were progressive too. There was certainly a punk aspect to the NWOBHM bands and it was the two sides of the coin as it were that inspired the young Ulrich.

Metal had started with Black Sabbath following on from the hard blues-tinged rock bands like The Who, The Kinks, Led Zeppelin and Cream and then it progressed to heavier heights with the second metal band (also from the Midlands), Judas

Priest. Hard rock bands Deep Purple and UFO were (are) not metal but they appealed to the same fanbase. Of course there were other subgenres such as glam rock with bands like T-Rex and Queen and Slade, The Sweet et al and prog rock with ELP, and in some ways they all had a major part to play in the development of metal and paved the way for the rise of American metal in the 1980s.

Punk came along in the mid-1970s and though largely popular in London and New York, this genre did manifest itself in the British provinces such as with the Bolton band Buzzcocks. The only American punk band to have any real affect on the British scene was the Ramones. The London scene spawned the likes of The Clash and the Sex Pistols, arguably the most famous punk bands of all time. Punk was more than just a style and type of music; it was a sub-culture; a fashion; a movement that impacted on Britain's disenfranchised and angst-ridden youth. The style of music has endured and manifested itself in various subgenres and fashions over the years. The anti-authoritarian punk attitude and DIY approach to releasing music had a fundamental impact on the NWOBHM bands, which in turn affected a certain young Danish born drummer. Ulrich was well-versed in music and it was primarily European rock and metal that he adored.

Lars Ulrich was born on December 26, 1963, in Gentofte, Denmark. He was raised in an upper-middle-class family. His father Torben was a well-known, respected and successful tennis player but his talents lay not only in the sports field: Torben was also a nifty jazz musician. Lars was surrounded by art, music, film and sport. He came from a cultural, high-brow family that inspired Lars to learn and appreciate new things. Lars Ulrich trained as a tennis player himself in his youth but in February, 1973, Lars was taken to a Deep Purple concert in Copenhagen by his father who had managed to get a handful of free passes (although as fate would have it one of his friends dropped out thus giving Lars the chance to attend instead). It's true to say the concert changed his life so much so that on the next day he bought Purple's now legendary *Fireball* album featuring the classic Purps line-up of singer Ian Gillan, guitarist Ritchie

Blackmore, bassist Roger Glover, organist Jon Lord and drummer Ian Paice. The album would become Lars' main reason for wanting to become a musician in a band rather than a sportsman. Aged twelve, his grandmother bought him a Ludwig drum kit; his first ever set of drums. Lars quickly became absorbed in hard rock and heavy metal, mostly British. These UK bands of the 1960s took the sound and feel of black American blues and made it heavier, grittier and ironically, introduced a generation of young Americans to the sound of black American blues which they had not previously appreciated. The British bands were white but they loved black music and the likes of The Who and The Kinks, then later Black Sabbath and Deep Purple led to Judas Priest and as such rock music got heavier. Much heavier; louder too. Aged sixteen, Lars and his family moved to Los Angeles to pursue his training as a tennis player. However, he was becoming increasingly obsessed by rock music and it was in America where he finally chose music over sport.

In 1981, the now aspiring drummer discovered a band from Stourbridge in the West Midlands (England) called Diamond Head. Their music owed a lot to Black Sabbath but it was faster and grittier. It was working-class metal. It was metal made for factory workers and kids uninterested in a life in academia. Ulrich had bought Diamond Head's debut *Lightning To The Nations* (released in 1980) and was so taken aback by the album that he travelled to London from California to see Diamond Head perform at the Woolwich Odeon on July 10, 1981. Though he loved the gig and was excited to be in London, Ulrich had not planned his visit properly and had nowhere to sleep. He managed to get backstage and Diamond Head's guitarist Brian Tatler and singer Sean Harris were so keen on the young Dane that they offered to let him stay at Tatler's house in the Midlands. Brian Tatler remembers, "We were all very impressed that he had flown all the way from America to see us! No one had ever done that before. His accent was very amusing and unusual, a mix of Danish/American."[v]

Ulrich toured with the band for a few weeks thereafter. "One of my enduring memories of that period is Lars and I staying up late at my parents' house in order to watch a video of Deep Purple at the California Jam 1974," says Tatler. "Lars would rave about Ritchie Blackmore and he would mime the guitar solos. He was and still is a huge music fan."[vi]

What Ulrich liked about Diamond Head's music was the way they used riffs; Diamond Head didn't go for the usual verse/chorus line-up in a song but they used middle breakdowns and developed different parts to songs rather than the standard three-part structure. The riffs by Diamond Head were monolithic and gritty; raw and powerful. They caught the attention of critics and metal bands but for various reasons did not make it into the commercially big league of metal players.

Back in the City Of Angels, the young Ulrich put an advertisement in a newspaper called *The Recycler* which read "Drummer looking for other metal musicians to jam with Tygers Of Pan Tang, Diamond Head and Iron Maiden". The advertisement received an answer from two guitarists from a band called Leather Charm that hailed from the LA area of southern California. Guitarists James Hetfield and Hugh Tanner were inspired by many of the hard rock and heavy metal bands that influenced Ulrich. Those bands included Deep Purple, Aerosmith, Queen, Ted Nugent and Motörhead. Many of Hetfield's influences leaned towards melody and structure rather than erratic riffs and aggressive melodies.

Speaking with the author, metal writer and fan Bob Nalbandian recalls his introduction to Lars Ulrich: "I first came across both Lars and James months before Metallica had formed. I grew up in Huntington Beach, CA (less than an hour south of Los Angeles) and Lars lived in Newport Beach in the early 1980s. My good friend Patrick Scott came across Lars from a *Recycler* ad he put out when he was looking to form a band. Both Patrick and I were totally into the NWOBHM scene and Lars' ad … caught Pat's attention. A couple of days later Patrick invited me to Lars' house (he lived in a condo with his parents) and we were freaking out on his amazing record collection! I had met James around the same time outside the local rock/metal club The Woodstock in Anaheim."[vii]

Nalbandian, who wrote for *The Headbanger* fanzine, wasn't too fond of Ulrich at first. "To be honest, he seemed like a spoiled, snotty kid when I first met him! [But] I hadn't really met many people from Europe at that time so it was kind of a new experience for me, he had a bit of that European sarcastic attitude which kind of put me off at first but I got to know and appreciate [it] later!"[viii]

James Hetfield was born in Downey, California on August 3, 1963 to amateur opera singer Cynthia and blue collar truck driver Virgil. Hetfield's siblings were from his mother's first marriage; two elder brothers and a younger sister. However, Hetfield's father left the family when his son was young and Cynthia and Virgil divorced in 1976. Hetfield's parents were both devoted Christian Scientists, a faith that prefers to opt for spiritual healing rather than conventional medicinal practices, even for example when Hetfield's mother was later dying of cancer. The faith respects conventional medicine but does not ordinarily use it. In 1979, when he was aged just sixteen, James Hetfield's mother died and he moved to his brother's house in Brea some twenty minutes drive from his home but he went back at weekends to jam with his buddies (Virgil Hetfield died in 1996 during Metallica's *Load* Tour). Hetfield was a keen music fan and had begun playing the piano around aged seven before he picked up some drum sticks. He started to play the drums on one of his brother's drum kits before he finally picked up a guitar aged fourteen. His fate was sealed.

As an adult, James Hetfield spoke to *Virginmega.com* about his classical musical lessons: "I did [take lessons] when I was about six or seven years old. My mother saw me banging on the piano once and mistakenly thought I was the next child prodigy, so she put me in some old lady's house after school to learn … I would have rather been out playing football with my buddies, but now I thank her every day for that because it developed my ear, and she made me sing at rehearsals as well, so I had to sing in public. I did read music for a while, but as time goes on, you forget things you don't use. I wish I had kept up with it, but it's not really necessary for us. It's all by ear. That's how I learned to play guitar, off playing records."[ix]

Hetfield was a huge fan of hard rock music particularly Aerosmith, Thin Lizzy, Deep Purple, AC/DC, Black Sabbath, Ted Nugent and KISS. He was also a huge fan of Steve Tyler, Aerosmith's iconic frontman. A couple of his earlier bands included Obsession (with guitarist/singer Jim Arnold, bassist/singer Ron Veloz and his brother Rich Veloz on drums) that turned out Sabbath, Zeppelin, Deep Purple and UFO covers while his next band Phantom Lord was formed with Hugh Tanner at Brea Olinda High School. They jammed and played covers but they did not play any gigs, ever. Hetfield recruited Ron McGovney to play bass even though he was a beginner. However, it is Leather Charm that is best known by most early Metallica fans...

Leather Charm was formed in June, 1981. The initial line-up featured singer James Hetfield, drummer Jim Mulligan, guitarist Hugh Tanner (who was later replaced by Troy James) and bassist Ron McGovney. They turned out covers by many of their favourite bands, including legendary British hard rockers Deep Purple whose album *Machine Head* was a major source of inspiration for most aspiring rock bands of the 1970s and 1980s regardless of nationality. Purple was formed in 1968 and while the band has had various line-ups over the years (even prior to the formation of Leather Charm) the most revered and commercially successful was undoubtedly singer Ian Gillan, guitarist Ritchie Blackmore, bassist Roger Glover, drummer Ian Paice and organist Jon Lord. This, the 'Mark II' line-up, created arguably some of the most famous and enduring hard rock albums of all time: *In Rock* (1970), *Fireball* (1971) and *Machine Head* (1972.) The latter certainly had a major impact on the evolution of metal with the classic songs 'Highway Star', 'Smoke On The Water' and 'Space Truckin'.

Leather Charm created an original song called 'Hit The Lights' but the outfit folded just months after it was formed. They also penned a couple of other tracks; one was called 'Handsome Ransom' and the other was named 'Let's Go Rock 'N' Roll' (elements of 'Let's Go Rock 'N' Roll' later morphed into the Metallica track 'No Remorse').

Ron McGovney: "We were doing kind of a glam thing, like, Sweet, and this British band called Girl (which featured Phil Lewis and Phil Collen), we did that song 'Hollywood Tease'. We did a bunch of covers as well like 'Pictured Life' from Scorpions, 'Wrathchild' and 'Remember Tomorrow' from Iron Maiden and 'Slick Black Cadillac' from Quiet Riot (the Randy Rhoads era)."[x]

Upon meeting each other in the fall of 1981 in Downey, California, Ulrich and Hetfield became fast friends through a shared love of rock and metal. "Certainly the first time Lars and I got together for a jam [forming a band] didn't happen, there was no vibe. And when he came to me with an opportunity to be on a record, that was pretty interesting. At that time in my life I wanted to play music, I didn't want to work."[xi]

Ulrich opened up a whole new world of metal for Hetfield and not only eagerly introduced him to some of the obscure NWOBHM bands but also other European metal outfits too. "I had heard of Iron Maiden and Def Leppard, but not too many of the other, more obscure, English metal bands," confessed Hetfield. "So when I first met up with Lars, I would spend days just going through his record collection, taping over my REO Speedwagon cassettes with bands like Angel Witch and Diamond Head and Motörhead. I was in heaven at his house."[xii]

Even though a band had not yet been officially formed, Ulrich got in touch with Metal Blade Records founder Brian Slagel about the possibility of recording a track for the upcoming metal compilation, *Metal Massacre*. The answer from Slagel was an affirmative nod of the head.

Brian Slagel told the author: "I was friends with Lars before he started Metallica. We were both into the NWOBHM and used to hang out and listen to music and search for it around LA. He always said he wanted to start a band. I started to put together a compilation album of local LA metal bands and Lars knew this. He mentioned if he had a band could they be on the album? I said yes and he and James recorded 'Hit The Lights' for it.[xiii]

"We were all young so we were just your typical manic metalheads! I was quite surprised how good it was considering

I was not sure how good a drummer Lars could be as I just knew him as a fan."[xiv]

In October, 1981, Ulrich formed a band with Hetfield and through Ulrich's close metal lovin' buddy Ron Quintana, Metallica was born.

Ron Quintana told the author of this book: "Lars and I met on top of Strawberry Hill on the island in the middle of Stow Lake in deepest Golden Gate Park at midnight or so one Friday night (or Saturday) in January, 1981. Our friends went there every weekend with ghetto blasters and tons of Budgie/Priest/Scorps/Maiden/Motörhead, etc; tapes to blast as loud as we wanted and not attract the cops (although they did trudge up there a time or two trying to catch us kids drinking and screamin' til 3a.m!). Lotsa cases of beer or other bottles and rarely a keg as it took so long to lug up there. Our East Bay buddy Rich Burch…actually met him first that day on Telegraph in Berkeley and… saw all the rare patches and buttons on his denim jacket! He invited Lars to our Banger Party and all of us quizzed him on all the NWOBHM bands he'd seen that we'd only heard about! His and my favourite band was Diamond Head at that moment so we hung out the most. Later, he drove me [and] then Rich home, but we talked metal in his huge brown AMC Pacer car (that is something of a joke to car enthusiasts) for hours! We hung out every time he visited north from Newport Beach through summer."[xv]

Quintana remembers the almost obsessive enthusiasm Ulrich had for heavy metal: "Lars was totally a metal fan and hardly ever mentioned tennis or his famous father 'til much later. We'd all collected any info in the Bay Area on the NWOBHM in 1979 and 1980 from *Sounds*, *NME* or *Melody Maker*. I immediately loved 'Am I Evil?' from a BBC recording as well as a London live recording from 1980 that featured my other favourite, 'Dead Reckoning'. Lars actually loved that tape (before I made him a copy) [so much] that he jammed my Fisher tape deck listening to the lyrics over and over one day he came to visit! I still have that broken wreck in the basement somewhere!"[xvi]

It was the band Diamond Head that most inspired the younger

Danish drummer. "Lars grew up with NWOBHM, 1979 in his travels between Copenhagen and [the] UK," says Quintana. "I liked the dramatically heavy riffs I first heard from Brian Tatler in 1980 [and] 1981."[xvii]

Diamond Head are such an integral part of the Metallica story that it's certainly worth giving a potted history of the cult Stourbridge metal band up to 1982 when Metallica had begun playing live and recording demos.

Diamond Head was formed in 1976 by high school mates Brian Tatler (guitars) and Duncan Scott (drums). Singer Sean Harris soon joined and the band adopted the name of Diamond Head derived from the 1975 Phil Manzanera album. The band eventually recruited their new bassist Colin Kimberley and they began playing shows. Their sets often consisted mostly of cover versions though they did pen their own material. They self-released a bunch of demos and even supported AC/DC and Iron Maiden. Diamond Head's influences included Black Sabbath and Judas Priest. With the New Wave Of British Heavy Metal in full swing but with no sign of getting signed to a major record label, they founded their own label, Happy Face Records and released the single 'Shoot Out The Lights' with the B-side 'Helpless' in 1980. Their now legendary debut *Lightning To The Nations* was initially released via Happy Face in 1980 and was only available via mail order for £3.50. The album includes such popular tracks as 'Am I Evil?', 'It's Electric' and 'Helpless'.

Brian Tatler: "The first album *Lightning To The Nations* is always the one people want to get hold of, it still pops up on eBay occasionally for £70 or sometimes more. There were two thousand copies of that pressed and sold. The early singles are quite rare, and the *Diamond Lights* EP because they all had a limited number of pressings, usually a thousand copies."[xviii]

With the success of their debut album they signed to MCA Records in 1981 and released the *Four Cuts* EP and then played at the 1982 Reading Festival. Their first MCA released album was 1982's *Borrowed Time* which included artwork by the revered fantasy artist Rodney Matthews, known for his work with Birmingham pomp rockers Magnum. It hit Number 24 in the

UK charts and the band launched a UK road trek in support of the acclaimed album. Those two albums plus the demos and singles releases were not only a major source of inspiration to Lars Ulrich and the rest of Metallica but also other metal bands on the West Coast scene.

With Lars Ulrich now determined to set the metal world alight with his new band, it would not be long before the name Metallica was created. The other name that was thrown around was Metal Mania which Quintana later used for his famed magazine.

Ron Quintana: "Lars and I joked about starting a record store/band/metal magazine together sometime; we each showed each other lists of names, I thought he liked 'Skull Orchard' best. I wasn't impressed with RedVette, TurboCharger, Lightning Vette or some of his list." Then Hetfield called to say he was jamming with some friends under the name Metallica; Ron recalled, 'I'd already started *Metal Mania* in August, 1981 so I didn't mind."[xix]

To get a powerful twin guitar sound that had made Judas

Priest's metal so distinctive Ulrich placed a second advertisement in *The Recycler* asking for another guitarist. Dave Mustaine answered the ad and was impressed by Ulrich's collection of nifty guitars and other bits of gear. Ulrich played Mustaine the 'Hit The Lights' demo but Mustaine wasn't all that impressed, thinking it needed more guitar solos. Mustaine convinced Ulrich that he should be in Metallica; Ulrich accepted and the band celebrated over some beers. Mustaine became Metallica's lead guitarist.

Dave Mustaine was born on September 13, 1961 in La Mesa, California to Emily and John Mustaine and was raised as a Jehovah's Witness. His turbulent teenage years had filtered him towards music, especially artists like Iron Maiden and Judas Priest et al. He also liked AC/DC, Led Zeppelin, The Beatles and acts like Cat Stevens and Elton John. "The music I liked was very eclectic. A lot of it was from the British Invasion. The guitar influence that affected my songwriting came from the NWOBHM. So I would have to say my whole style is supported around the whole blues thing, and going into making a thrash style…" Mustaine's own life story is remarkable; when he was in his teenage years, he began to increasingly turn to musical creativity: "There was a lot of pain and a lot of anger that was coming out through my guitar playing."[xx]

Mustaine was in awe of those bands so much so he picked up an electric guitar (a B.C. Rich) and began playing in the 1970s. Mustaine explained his reasons for getting into music: "I liked playing music and I liked the lifestyle that went along with it if you were in a band. Because it was kind of like you are in a gang… It was fun for me... It was really cool to experience travelling and meeting people, and playing in front of people around the world."[xxi]

Prior to joining Metallica, Mustaine was in a band called Panic which he left to join Ulrich and Hetfield's metal venture. Things would never be quite the same again for any of them from this point onwards.

Metal fan Bob Nalbandian who wrote for the metal mag *The Headbanger* says, "I really dug Dave Mustaine in Metallica. [In my opinion] when he first joined he was really the only truly accomplished musician; Lars was just starting out on drums and James was only singing at the time; he didn't really find his vocal identity until much later (around *Ride The Lightning*). But I thought Dave really added the driving fuel and brash attitude that really carried the band over the top."[xxii]

Metallica were working straight jobs while trying to get their band off the ground as bassist Ron McGovney explained to Pat O' Connor at *Shockwaves* some years later: "We would all get together after work. James wasn't working at the time and Lars was working a graveyard shift at a 24-hour gas station, and Dave was... self-employed. At the time it was just Dave playing guitar and James was just singing. It got to the point where James had said that he didn't think he was too good of a singer and he only wanted to play rhythm guitar. So we found this singer named Sammy DeJohn who was in a local band called Ruthless – he rehearsed with us for about three weeks but we never played a show with him … James went back to singing again."[xxiii]

With the newly hired bassist Ron McGovney of Hetfield's former band Leather Charm, Metallica played their initial live show at Radio City in Anaheim, California on March 14, 1982. James Hetfield: "There were a lot of people there, maybe 200, because we had all my school friends and all Lars' and Ron's and Dave's buddies. I was really nervous and a little uncomfortable without a guitar and then during the first song Dave broke a string. It seemed to take him an eternity to change it and I was standing there really embarrassed. We were really disappointed afterwards. But there were never as many people at the following shows as there were at that first one."[xxiv]

The band's first ever live set-list looked like this: 'Hit The Lights', 'Blitzkrieg', 'Helpless', 'Jump In The Fire', 'Let It Loose', 'Sucking My Love', 'Am I Evil?', 'The Prince' and 'Killing Time'. McGovney's impressions of Ulrich's drumming skills were not exactly favourable but with the new line-up amendments they started jamming straight away. McGovney was a budding photographer at the time, often seen taking his camera into gigs and photographing bands live. Ron McGovney: "I knew James

[Hetfield] in junior high but didn't really start hanging out with him till our freshman year in high school... they started getting me into hard rock, I had been into Foreigner and Boston... bands like that, but then they got me into bands like UFO. I started taking acoustic guitar lessons when I was a fourteen, a freshman in high school."[xxv]

On March 27, 1982, Metallica supported the New Wave Of British Heavy Metal band Saxon fronted by Biff Byford at the

Whisky A-Go-Go in LA. It was only Metallica's second live show. McGovney was enquiring about getting Metallica to support Saxon for one of the two shows they were playing there when he bumped into Tommy Lee and Vince Neil of Mötley Crüe. Glam metal band Crüe were fast becoming a very popular band in the LA area with the likes of fellow hair metal band Ratt, so they didn't want to support Saxon but Ratt did on the first night. McGovney was introduced to the booking lady – who thought Metallica sounded like the Oregon glam metal band Black 'N Blue – by the Crüe guys and got Metallica to support Saxon on the second night. Writing in the *LA Times* on March 29, journalist Terry Atkinson said of Metallica: "Saxon could also use a fast, hot guitar player of the Eddie Van Halen ilk. Opening quartet Metallica had one, but little else. The local group needs considerable development to overcome a pervasive awkwardness."

Around this period Hetfield was working at the Steven Label Corporation in Santa Fe Springs doing a mind-numbing job of making stickers while dreaming about rock 'n' roll success. Ulrich – who lived in Newport Beach – was still at high school and commuted to Norwalk to play with the rest of the band.

The seeds were quickly being sown.

Prior to what is considered to be the first line-up of Metallica (singer/guitarist James Hetfield, drummer Lars Ulrich, guitarist Dave Mustaine and bassist Ron McGovney), the fledgling band experimented with various guitar and vocal sounds, creating a combination which was essentially the same as Diamond Head's. The band really wanted to have a frontman like their heroes Iron Maiden and Deep Purple.

Lars Ulrich told *Metal Forces'* Bernard Doe in 1984: "We've auditioned over fifty vocalists, listened to hundreds of demos from others, but we still haven't found anyone to fit in with what we were doing. The only person that we thought may fit in was John Bush of Armored Saint, but he apparently doesn't want to do it."[xxvi] The band also considered Jess Cox from the English band Tygers Of Pan Tang but nothing came of that idea.[xxvii]

It was thought within the band that Hetfield's vocals were too extreme for the fans. Metallica wanted to be a five-piece but that meant finding a frontman to fill the gap; their heroes like Judas Priest and Iron Maiden had very distinct frontmen but when the band decided to keep Hetfield as both the rhythm guitarist and lead singer it meant that he had to start writing lyrics because all of his favourite singers wrote lyrics. He felt at first that it didn't matter what he sang about but over time he became a more confident singer and began to take the art of writing lyrics much more seriously.

On May 25, Metallica played at Ulrich's school, Backbay High School in Costa Mesa in front of a small audience of non-metal fans; perhaps not surprisingly the gig didn't really work out too well for them. Then on June 5 they returned to the venue where they played their first ever gig at Anaheim's Radio City.

'Hit The Lights' was recorded for the aforementioned *Metal Massacre* collection – the first Metallica recording – with Hetfield also taking on bass duties while local player Lloyd Grant played a guitar lead (on later pressings all the guitars were played by Mustaine).

"I remember the day I went over to Lars' house, he said, 'Check out this song,' and he played me 'Hit The Lights'," Grant told metal fan and writer Bob Nalbandian in 1997. "We were both into that heavy kind of shit. He wanted me to play some guitar leads on it but I couldn't make it over to Ron McGovney's house to do the recording so James and Lars brought the four-track over to my apartment and I did the solo on a little Montgomery Ward amp."[xxviii]

What was the reason for the talented Lloyd Grant's brief tenure in Metallica? "I had several disappointments with previous bands I was in, I guess that's my reason for not pursuing Metallica," he explained. "There were a lot of flaky musicians; however, this was not the case with Lars, he was 100% intense with the music."[xxix]

This was obviously the very early stages of the band and more players were evidently needed. Annoyingly, when the collection was finally released on June 14, 1982, the band's name was misspelled 'Mettallica'. However, the band managed to use this glaring error to their advantage by using it to publicise their name further.

The first proper Metallica demo (though never officially released) that the band recorded was called *Power Metal*, which initially had Hetfield singing like Sean Harris from Diamond Head but he amended his vocals to make himself sound rougher (An obscure demo called *Ron McGovney's 82 Garage Demo* was never released though it does contain 'Hit The Lights' and 'Jump In The Fire' while the rest of the eight-track demo was made up of cover songs from Sweet Savage and Diamond Head. It was recorded on March 14, 1982 in McGovney's garage and preceded the *Power Metal* demo by a few weeks). *Power Metal* was recorded in April, 1982 in McGovney's garage. It contained four original songs: 'Hit The Lights', 'Jump In The Fire', 'The Mechanix' and 'Motorbreath'. Ulrich and his buddy Pat Scott personally mailed copies of their demos to as many record companies around the world as they could afford.

How the demo came to be called *Power Metal* is a funny story: Ron went to make some business cards to send to promoters and music industry people when they mailed out the tape, and the card was intended to just have the band's name, logo and phone number. But Ron thought that looked too plain and wanted to try to sum up their sound too; declining to use 'hard rock' or 'heavy metal' he used the term 'Power Metal'.

The gigs rolled on: the band played one gig with Brad Parker (also known as Damian C. Phillips) at the Concert Factory on July 3 in Costa Mesa but it didn't work out and Parker moved on to other bands, notably Odin. On July 15, they played at a party in Huntington Beach and on August 2 Eric Carr of KISS attended Metallica's show at The Troubadour in Hollywood, then, after playing with Steeler and Sound Barrier at the Whisky, Metallica returned to The Troubadour to play with Ratt on August 18; they played their first ever encore that night. More gigs followed in the LA area throughout the summer of 1982 before they ventured up north to play yet more shows.

Photographer Bill Hale remembers the first time he shot Metallica: "That would be September 18, 1982 at The Stone in

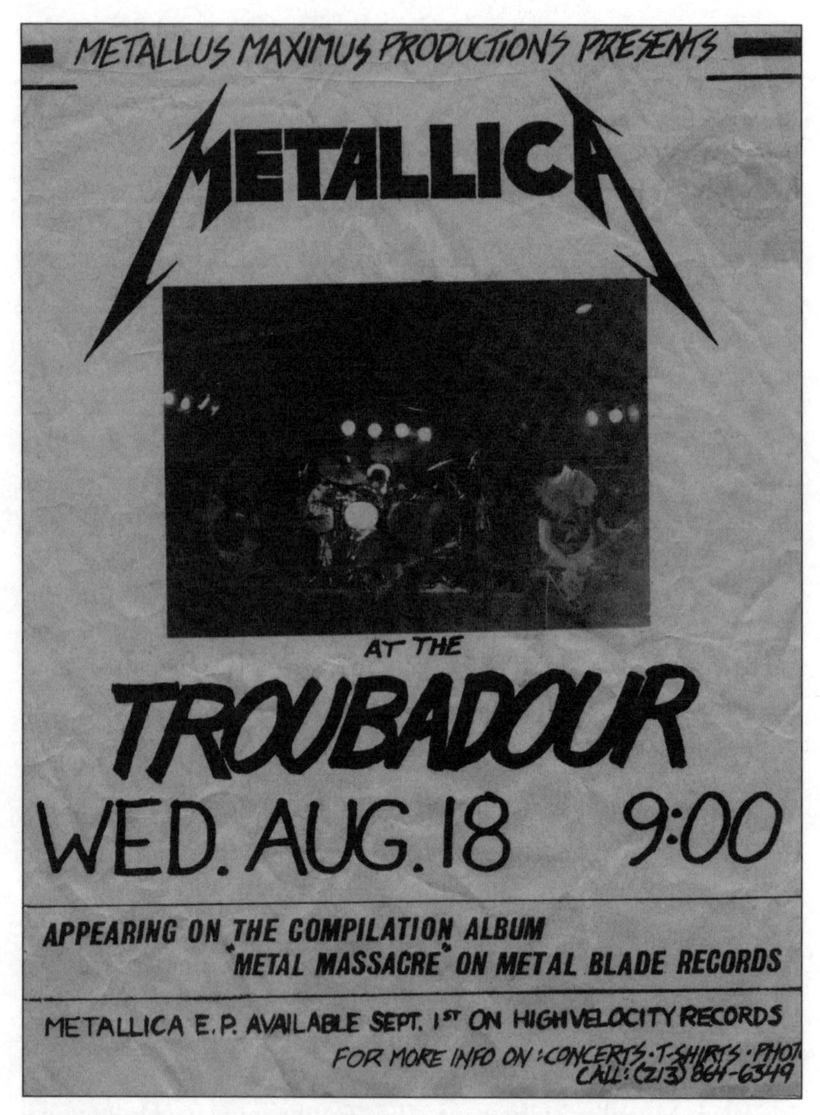

San Francisco. [Importantly] that would also be the band's first gig in the Bay Area. We (John Strednansky – editor and chief of *Metal Rendezvous* magazine) knew Lars before he had started the band! Lars and Stred met up and Lars would call us at the *MRV* offices… We heard 'Hit The Lights' as it was coming together, over the phone!"[xxx]

Reviewing the band's show with a crowd of two hundred people at The Stone, Brian Lew wrote in the fanzine *Whiplash*:

"The heaviest band in the U.S. of A., Metallica, rampaged into the City By The Bay and spread more havoc than the 1906 earthquake!"

However, even though McGovney had an important role to play in the early stages of Metallica's career, Ulrich and Hetfield were soon to change their minds about the line-up but not before more demos were made: *No Life 'Til Leather* was released in July. It was the band's first officially released demo and their most widely-circulated one too. It would have a major impact on the band's subsequent debut album.

Brian Ross of the NWOBHM band Blitzkrieg told the author: "My first brush with Metallica was way back when I was doing a bit of A&R work at Neat Records in Newcastle [England]. Lars had sent a copy of the *No Life 'Til Leather* demo to Neat. They were after a deal with the label that had all their favourite NWOBHM bands on it. Dave Wood, the M.D. at Neat, gave me a pile of demos to listen to, among them the Metallica one. What immediately struck me was that here was an American band that sounded like a NWOBHM band. I was quite impressed by them."[xxxi] Ultimately, despite Brian's positive reaction, the band was not offered a deal by Neat.

In the end, *No Life 'Til Leather*, their latest demo, was funded by Kenny Kane for an imprint of Rocshire Records called High Velocity in Orange County. It was recorded at an eight-track studio called Chateau East in Tustin. However, the label was proudly punk-oriented and Kane was not a big fan of the material when he heard the demo, so the band self-released it. *Metal Up Your Ass Live* was recorded thereafter at the Old Waldorf in San Francisco on November 29.

The demos quickly became sought-after items amongst metal tape trading collectors. Even though some fans complained that Metallica were too fast to be a metal band or even too punk, they offered something new and vibrant. Bernard Doe who went on to co-found and edited the (sadly now defunct) UK magazine *Metal Forces* comments, "Metallica were already having a big influence on the underground metal scene. Now, absolutely no one, if they're being honest, could have predicted just how popular Metallica would become at that point, but it was clear even then that they were extending the boundaries of heavy metal and spearheading something very special."[xxxii]

The band was beginning to look promising though relations were sometimes strained between certain members. Over the years many anecdotes have been recalled from this period much to either the amusement or bemusement of Metallica fans although it has to be noted that they are fairly typical rock 'n' roll stories, disagreements, fights, arguments. Internal tensions mounted.

McGovney was growing tired of what he felt was the band's apparent lack of organisation and suggested they hire a manager to help them with bookings and such. McGovney complained about the awkward situation to *Shockwaves'* Pat O' Connor in 1997: "I was really getting sick of the situation. And I didn't know why this was happening because I did what I could and what they asked me to do. Lars and I butted heads a lot, I hate when people show up late and use you all the time and that's just what Lars did. I would have to drive all the way down to Newport Beach to pick him up, so I told him, 'If you can't make it, it's not my problem.'"[xxxiii] There were also frequent arguments over money …

Still, the Ulrich/Hetfield/Mustaine/McGovney line-up of the band was becoming a powerful force to be reckoned with on the live front. Then *Kerrang!* journalist Xavier Russell recalls the first interview he ever did as a writer for that magazine: "Mötley Crüe and Metallica both on the same day in San Francisco, 1982. You couldn't get two more different bands. The Crüe were just rowdy noisy party animals who were more interested in getting laid than listening to me waffling on about the brilliance and rawness of their album *Too Fast For Love*, while Metallica were the total opposite. Here was a band that would talk for hours about Iron Maiden, Saxon, Venom and the like. They really did take their music seriously, that doesn't mean to say they didn't like to get wasted – they did, and their tipple back then was Carlsberg Elephant and frozen Absolute Vodka!"[xxxiv]

More specifically, Russell says, "I first came across Metallica quite by accident. The year was 1982, I was in Concorde, California doing a piece and live review of Mötley Crüe who were just breaking big. A metalhead by the name of Ron Quintana who ran the underground fanzine *Metal Mania*, thrust the now legendary *No Life 'Til Leather* demo into my grubby mits. I ignored the demo for a few days, and then got continually hassled by Ron asking if I'd played it yet. I finally gave it a spin and was totally blown away. I'd never heard anything quite like it before. The rawness, the speed of the songs and the sheer energy all combined to make Metallica the next big thing.

"As luck would have it they were due to play a 'Metal Monday' at the legendary Old Wardorf set in San Francisco's financial district! The power and brutal music Metallica played that hot sweaty night very nearly started an earthquake, the nearby Pyramid Building was swaying to the thunderous chords of 'The Four Horsemen'. This was Metallica Mark II: Ron McGovney (bass), James Hetfield (guitar), Lars Ulrich (drums) and Dave Mustaine (guitar). What was so refreshing about the band back then was their sheer energy, enthusiasm and brutal speed. I'd never seen anything quite like it, the power and adrenalin was amazing, the sweat flew off the stage as Messrs Hetfield and Mustaine went into battle. Both were very similar in look and style, but it did feel like they were trying to push each other out of the way and hog the limelight – needless to say Hetfield eventually won! I got talking to them after the show, and they were more interested in talking about Saxon and Venom than me asking them about the current state of the LA metal scene!

"I did end up interviewing the band for *Kerrang!* and the piece was entitled *'M.U.Y.A' – (Metal Up Your Ass!)* It was the first time Metallica had been properly covered by the European press, apart from an article in *Metal Forces*."[xxxv]

On said line-up, Brian Slagel told the author of this book: "Well, I knew Lars the best since we were friends before Metallica started. Great kid who was super hyper and like me a big time fan. So we got along well and always have. James was pretty shy in the early days, so we did not talk a whole lot in the beginning but a really good guy always. Ron was a cool guy as well, really kind of a regular guy so to speak. Mustaine, I think had rock star in him from the early days. He was great when sober but he could out drink us all. He was such a great player too, much better than anyone around at that time. I always got along well with Dave as well. All really good guys to this day even!"[xxxvi]

One night Ulrich and Hetfield went to a gig by Californian band Trauma at the iconic West Hollywood drinking hole Whisky A-Go-Go. A bassist by the name of Cliff Burton stunned Ulrich and Hetfield; meanwhile, tensions with McGovney were not improving and eventually he separated from the band in December and thus Burton was invited to join Metallica. They caught up with Burton the following night at The Troubadour.

Hetfield recalled an anecdote about the show to *Metal Hammer* in 1999: "We had got our first encore ever and we went backstage and agreed that we were going to play this song and he [Lars] went into something else which we hadn't rehearsed in months and months. I didn't know the lyrics, so we just muddled our way through it and after he got up from his drum riser I just slugged him really hard in the stomach and said, 'Don't ever fucking do that again!' There have been a few times where I have felt like using my size against him, but he gets the picture most of the time."[xxxvii]

Hetfield effectively had to choose the band over his friend, McGovney. "I don't think at the time it had anything to do with my musicianship because I was basically playing what they asked me to play," McGovney later said. "James showed me what to play and I played it. I understood the camaraderie between James and Lars as far as writing goes and I didn't want to infiltrate that."[xxxviii]

After about three shows in San Francisco in total, McGovney played one of his last gigs with Metallica in November, 1982 at Mabuhay Gardens and then his final appearance with Metallica was at The Old Waldorf on November 29 where they recorded the now famous *Live Metal Up Your Ass* demo. A month or so later McGovney sold all his equipment and quit the rock scene. "I would have been better off as a paid road manager rather than the bass player … But like I said, that's all history..."[xxxix]

After initially declining to join this thirsty young metal band,

Cliff Burton had a change of heart and offered them one stipulation at the end of 1982: that they move to El Cerrito in the San Francisco Bay Area, Burton's home town. Burton wanted nothing to do with the superficial LA scene and he was growing tired of Trauma and wanted a change. "They were starting to adopt these attitudes..." Burton reflected in February, 1986, "well, it was starting to get a little commercial in different ways, just different general musical attitudes that I found annoying."[xl]

Lars Ulrich's buddy and fellow metal maniac, Brian Slagel, recalls, "I saw him [Burton] first when he was in the band Trauma who were on *Metal Massacre 2*. They played a show in LA and he was incredible. Lars mentioned to me they were looking for a bass player and I told him he should come see Cliff. As soon as he and James saw him, Lars told me that guy would be in Metallica and sure enough he soon was."[xli]

The band readily agreed to Burton's request as they were über-keen to have Burton in the band so they packed up and moved north. Photographer Bill Hale says, "We were all just trying to live the metal dream. The Bay Area had a great scene already. Think 1960s and the 1970s, so the clubs where there, the press was there and when my generation came of age... We just inherited this huge musical legacy. Ya know [Ron] Quintana had his mag [*Metal Mania*] going, we were right behind him. There was a ton of fucking cool record shops and fans who dug metal! There was a big thing going on when Metallica happened up the state from LA. They really just found a home here but you have to keep in mind, there was a ton of bands! Metallica just played harder, faster and louder!"[xlii]

Cliff Burton was born on February 10, 1962, in Castro Valley, California. He was close to his parents Jan and Ray and to his elder brother Scott and sister Connie. Though he was initially being given piano lessons after being introduced to classical music by his father, Burton picked up a bass aged thirteen and his interest in rock and heavy metal deepened. This came after the early death of his brother.

His mother, Jan Burton, said: "He said to a couple of people, 'I'm gonna be the best bassist for my brother.'[xliii] At first, his parents were naturally unsure if he was talented but encouraged him nonetheless and enrolled him in lessons. After about six months, the fruits of his labours started to show, as his mother continued: 'I thought, 'This kid's got real potential,' and I was totally amazed 'cause none of the kids in our family had any musical talent!' At school Cliff took yet more lessons from a jazz bassist, who introduced him to Bach, Beethoven and baroque, as well as how to read sheet music. Cliff was collating an enviable amalgam of influences and talent.

Burton's influences soon ranged from Geddy Lee of Rush to Black Sabbath's Geezer Butler to Phil Lynott of Thin Lizzy and the jazz musician Stanley Clarke. Certainly the way Lemmy of Motörhead used distortion had an effect on Burton who practiced for hours each day aspiring to be like his idols.

In fact, Motörhead was a major source of inspiration to all the members of Metallica. Motörhead was formed in 1975 by bassist/singer Ian "Lemmy" Kilmister after being fired from working with Hawkwind. But from that point, Lemmy forged a legendary rock career. Back in the late 1970s and even to this day, Motörhead are one of those rare bands that appeal not only to metal fans because of the heaviness of the music but also to punk fans because of the aggression, speed and grit of the songs.

The trio of *Overkill* (1979), *Bomber* (1979) and *Ace Of Spades* (1980) had a massive impact on the American metal bands of the early 1980s, including Metallica. Joel McIver – author of the book *Motörhead Over The Top* – says that Metallica were chiefly inspired by the English band because of "the aggression and speed of the music, as well as Lemmy's image and refusal to dilute his message."[xliv]

Indeed, the way Lemmy played his bass was totally unique; like the sound of military ammunition. He plays the bass like a lead guitar which often confuses those who are not familiar with the band's ongoing music. They were often not popular with critics – though it has changed now – yet they have a loyal fanbase that has kept the band afloat for over thirty years. The band has had various line-up changes over the past few decades with the only constant member being Lemmy – the most revered line-up was probably with guitarist Fast Eddie Clarke and drummer Philthy Animal Taylor. The famous Motörhead icon Snaggletooth is one of the most recognised symbols in metal along with Iron Maiden's mascot Eddie and the Judas Priest symbol which is commonly known as the 'Devil's Tuning Fork'. Members of Metallica loved the merchandise – mainly T-shirts in the early days – that the likes of Motörhead and Iron Maiden produced and distributed.

All these influences weighed heavily on the young Cliff Burton; he formed his first outfit EZ-Street during his tenure as a student at Castro Valley High School. EZ-Street had a couple of players who would later go on to have notable careers of their own: drummer Mike Bordin from Faith No More and Ozzy Osbourne's solo band and "Big" Jim Martin, also from Faith No More. The name EZ-Street derived from a topless bar in the Bay Area. Burton and his buddy Martin formed a second band together called Agents Of Misfortune whilst studying at Chabot College in Hayward, California. They entered a 'Battle Of The Bands' contest at the Hayward Area Recreation Department which was filmed on video tape (the video in question contains Burton's riffs for what would become Metallica's '(Anesthesia) Pulling Teeth' and 'For Whom The Bell Tolls').

In 1982, Burton became a member of Trauma who later contributed a track called 'Such A Shame' to the *Metal Massacre, Vol 2* compilation. Trauma were especially keen on Iron Maiden and Montrose, the hard rock band fronted by Sammy Hagar who later found fame as David Lee Roth's replacement in the Californian rock band Van Halen. Hagar would become one of the most iconic frontmen in American rock.

The common thread that tied them together was – yet again – a mutual love of the NWOBHM and a love of hard rock bands from the 1960s and 1970s. Saxon's Biff Byford told the author in an interview: "British heavy metal was a big influence on them. I know Dave Mustaine as well; obviously he was in Metallica at that time as well. A lot of young American bands at that time were looking for a less commercial approach."[xlv]

The Saxon albums *Saxon*, *Wheels Of Steel*, *Strong Arm Of The*

Leather and *Denim And Leather* (all released between 1979 and 1981) are benchmarks in British heavy metal and while they struggled to find success in America, serious American metal enthusiasts like Lars Ulrich sought out those early albums via import stores. Saxon were one of the major players in the NWOBHM movement and while they never received the heights of success afforded to Iron Maiden and Def Leppard – whose influences were not metal but glam rock and whose music was not heavy but melodic – Saxon retained a loyal following and their music and legacy endures to this day. Songs like 'Wheels Of Steel', '747 (Strangers In The Night)', 'Motorcycle Man', 'Heavy Metal Thunder' and '20,000 Ft' are classic heavy metal tracks and the fact that Saxon never shied away from being labeled a metal band especially appealed to members of Metallica. Metal fans often talk about the impact Diamond Head and Motörhead had on the early sound of Metallica but the fact is Saxon had just as much of an influence. The relentless riffing, pounding drums, decisive melodies and the gruff but oddly melodic vocals of Biff Byford have become synonymous with British heavy metal. Unknown to many but adored by serious metal enthusiasts, Saxon are one of Britain's greatest metal treasures. Ulrich loved them.

Moving on, Metal Blade Records founder, rock scribe and NWOBHM fan Brian Slagel recalls, "Metallica was too heavy for the LA scene once they started playing out live. That was one of the reasons they moved to SF. Metallica actually played mostly covers at first. Their set had 'Hit The Lights' and then Diamond Head, Blitzkreig and Holocaust covers."[xlvi]

Metal writer and fan Bob Nalbandian who witnessed the creation of Metallica says, "They were obviously much faster and much more European influenced as far as their music goes, which we loved. When they first started out playing the OC [Orange County] and LA clubs they were performing primarily covers of Diamond Head, Sweet Savage, Blitzkrieg, etc., but nobody (except for people like Pat [Scott] and I) knew that they were covers since those bands were obscure here in the US. They performed well in Orange County but they definitely didn't fit in with the LA club scene, which was heavily glam at the time."[xlvii]

Since the autumn months of 1982, Metallica had been making regular trips up to San Francisco from LA and were excited about the reaction and the size of crowds they were playing to. Lars Ulrich said: "We never really got on with the LA audiences too well, we had a loyal 200 or so people, but it never really spread beyond that. In the early days LA was still very much poser and glam and we were really the first band to do something different from all the Mötley Crüe, Ratt and Steeler-sounding bands."[xlviii]

Metallica were described by a lot of their LA peers as an almost punk-like band but the fact is Metallica were trying something new; something that set them apart from the LA posers and glammed-up pampered poodle-haired bands. Metallica lived and breathed the music – it wasn't about image. Hell, it wasn't even about the women musicians attracted either. They were metal nerds.

"I think a lot of the persona did develop out of where we came from," Hetfield explained to writer Greg Pratt. "The speed, the intensity, the loudness, we wanted the attention. Growing up in Los Angeles playing with all the glam bands when the scene was all about looks, hair, whatever, and we were certainly not about that, we wanted music, we had to play louder, faster, for people to notice us."[xlix]

It's interesting even by this point in their history to look back and see how they'd progressed as a live band. "[Initially] they were definitely pretty amateurish," remembers *The Headbanger* fanzine writer and metal fan Bob Nalbandian. "I saw their first show at Radio City (small club in Anaheim next door to The Woodstock) and I saw their second show opening for Saxon at the Whisky (which was quite a leap!). Like I said, they played eighty percent cover songs (I think only two originals). But they developed rather quickly. I think one of the last shows they played before moving up to San Francisco was opening for Y&T at The Woodstock and I really noticed the band [had] improved immensely. James was playing rhythm guitar at that point and that's when I first really saw the true potential for Metallica to make it big."[l]

With Burton onboard in late 1982 and with the band fully settled in a new home, Metallica were about to embark on a major change in their burgeoning career. Metallica and Cliff Burton biographer Joel McIver says, "At first Cliff and Dave Mustaine were the musical prodigies of the band. James learned a lot from them about music theory and Lars learned about songwriting and arranging. But they all listened to a lot of non-metal stuff anyway, from U2 to Peter Gabriel to Skynyrd."[li]

The seeds had been sown and they were on the verge of some major developments happening in their career. With Ulrich's passion and drive, Hetfield's enthusiasm and Mustaine and Burton's sense of music and knowledge of music theory, Metallica would enter the most creative period of their career and arguably their greatest era.

Kill 'Em All
1983

"I honestly believe that the kids who are into the Priest, Maiden, KISS, Sister thing will take into what we're doing. I'm not saying it's something that's going to happen overnight, but it could gradually start developing and Metallica could be the front runners of a new branch of heavy metal."

Lars Ulrich[lii]

After Ulrich, Hetfield and Mustaine moved to sound engineer Mark Whitaker's house at 3132 Carlson Boulevard in El Cerrito in February 1983, the first time the newly amended line-up of the band played together in front of an audience was on March 5 at a club called The Stone, while in the same month they recorded their first demo – *Megaforce* – with their recently acquired bassist, Cliff Burton.

Indeed, with their live reputation growing with each gig, they were eager to begin work on their first album but Metal Blade Records were not in a position to finance it. The tape attracted the interest of one label, Rocshire Records, but the band could sense that something was afoot. "We had been playing that tape to some different people and the response we had got was so overwhelming that we decided to wait and see what could happen," Lars Ulrich told *Metal Forces'* Bernard Doe. "Anyway the people at Rocshire didn't really know too much about what was going on with HM [heavy metal]. So we shopped around and talked to Firesign, the people that handle Riot, Mike Varney at Shrapnel and Brian Slagel's Metal Blade."[liii]

However, help was just around the corner. Jonny 'Z' Zazula, a concert promoter, had heard the demo tape *No Life 'Til Leather* and tried to help Metallica get a deal with some New York labels rather than the LA area (Cliff Burton is credited on *No Life 'Til*

Leather but he did not actually play on the demo). Unable to get a deal, Zazula got some cash together to fund the album himself and consequently signed Metallica to his own label Megaforce Records, which he founded specifically for Metallica's release(s). Zazula was also the owner of New Jersey's famed record store Rock 'N' Roll Heaven where they would import many foreign metal releases, mostly European. He was a fundamental figure in the East Coast metal scene.

Metallica relocated to The Old Bridge in Queens, New York. They slept in their rehearsal area at a place called the Music Building and members of the thrash band Anthrax gave them a toaster and a refrigerator. Where Metallica slept was basically a dingy storage area. Times were hard.

However, all was not as it seemed. Members of the band were becoming increasingly frustrated with Mustaine, internal tensions were sky high and the personality clashes seemed irreparable. "Dave Mustaine was really the face of the band. James was the lead singer but Mustaine did all the connecting with the fans from the stage, because James was still incredibly shy. Mustaine was certainly a character, but it just became too much for the rest of us … it just stopped becoming fun. That outweighed any fear we had of replacing him."[liv]

Relationships between Hetfield and Mustaine during 1982 to 1983 were especially fragile. Lars Ulrich explained in 1984: "I think James [Hetfield] and I always thought that the initial line-up of Ron [McGovney] on bass and Dave [Mustaine] on lead guitar wasn't people [*sic*] who we were going to take all the way."[lv]

On April 1, 1983, Ulrich and Hetfield hired guitarist Kirk Hammett from the thrash metal band Exodus that had previously supported Metallica. Metallica's soundman was the manager of Exodus at the time and introduced the band to Hammett. Was this fate? "I remember the first time I heard Kirk," enthused Ulrich. "He had a feel that very few young players have – very rooted in European metal. It was really nice to hear an American guy who didn't play like Eddie Van Halen."[lvi]

Just ten days later on April 11, Mustaine was out of the band as they were just beginning session work for their upcoming album. Mustaine's last gig with Metallica was on the Saturday at The Rods and then on the following Monday the band packed up and loaded Mustaine's gear into a car and drove him to Port Authority Bus Terminal. Mustaine was sent home on a four-day bus journey from the East Coast to the West Coast. On the journey back to LA Mustaine wrote down some lyrics on a muffin wrapper which became the song 'Set The World Afire' ('Set The World Afire' appears on the Megadeth album *So Far, So Good…So What!* from 1988). There would be a lot of animosity and public feuds between Mustaine – who very much went on to find success on his own terms – and the guys in Metallica for quite some time (On their debut album *Killing Is My Business… And Business Is Good*, Megadeth would record the Metallica demo 'The Mechanix' as 'Mechanix' from the *No Life 'Til Leather* tape which Metallica recorded and renamed 'The Four Horsemen' for *Kill 'Em All)*.

Ron Quintana – a close buddy of Lars Ulrich and a metal anorak who founded the cult magazine, *Metal Mania* – told the author of this book: "When they kicked Dave out in April, I really thought it changed their dynamic and didn't expect them to ever be huge, until about the *Master Of Puppets* tour [Damage, Inc. Tour, 1986 to 1987] then I realised there was no stopping them!"[lvii]

Metallica just wanted to be a recording band and go out and tour and play sweaty clubs around the States and maybe one day, the world, but they soon learned that the politics of band life and record companies would get in the way. Learning how to compromise in a band was no easy feat.

Photographer Bill Hale told the author: "Mustaine was cool! Where James was shy and did not talk much, Dave was a riot! I went on to photograph Dave for most of the 1980s. We got to be good friends... They all drank, we all drank…"[lviii]

Metallica's first show with their new lead guitarist was at The Showcase in Drover, New Jersey on April 16, just a few days after Mustaine left for LA. Hammett learned the Metallica set-list in just four days. This personnel change would alter the landscape of the band's sound and Hammett's skill on the fretboard was immediately apparent to even the most enthusiastic of Metallica fans. Ulrich and Hetfield knew right away that they had made the right choice in hiring Hammett who was not only a very professional player but also supremely talented. They hit it off right away. Hammett brought a new aspect to the band's sound.

Kirk Hammett was born on November 18, 1962 in San Francisco. Hammett is of both Filipina (from his mother) and Irish (from his father) descent. Hammett went to De Anza High School in Richmond, California where he made friends with Les Claypool, later of Primus fame. Such was Hammett's dedication to playing the guitar that he took a soul-destroying job at Burger King to save up enough cash to buy a Marshall Amp; needless to say he quit the poorly paid vocation once he bought his cherished item. Some of his earliest guitars included a copy of a 1978 Fender Stratocaster and a 1974 Gibson Flying V. Growing up in northern California, Hammett adored KISS, Aerosmith, Led Zeppelin and Jimi Hendrix. He was into bands where there was a distinctive guitar edge to their sound. He loved to hear the crazy fretboard wizardry of Hendrix at his most raw or Jimmy Page's wild solos especially on live bootlegs.

In 1980, Kirk Hammett formed Exodus, one of the most important and influential thrash metal bands of the Bay Area, with singer Paul Baloff. They both met at a house party in North Berkeley. Initially they got together with guitarist Tim Agnello, bassist Carlton Melson and drummer Tom Hunting. However, once the band had been christened Exodus, there would be some changes to the line-up: Hammett's guitar tech Gary Holt replaced Agnello and bassist Jeff Andrews took over from Melson. The band would merge their punk and metal influences together creating one furious melting pot of aggressive riffs and fierce vocals. The only recording Hammett made whilst in Exodus was a 1982 demo tape (Hammett would later be replaced by Rick Hunolt).

By now, Metallica was a name that could not be avoided in the Bay Area. Kirk Hammett told rock writer Jaan Uhelszki: "I was familiar with their music before I joined the band. Exodus played with Metallica quite a bit, so I knew the songs. I had the *No Life 'Til Leather* demo and listened to it quite a bit. It was what everyone in the San Francisco underground metal scene was listening to in 1982."[lix]

When Hammett joined Metallica he was taking guitar lessons from the fretboard wizard Joe Satriani. Hammett first visited Satriani at his music store in Berkeley called Secondhand Guitars. Friends of Hammett immediately picked up on the difference in Hammett's playing since he had been taking guitar lessons. Hammett had learned more about technique and style and discovered how not to compromise sound but to embrace experimentation and innovation. Satriani liked Hammett from the get-go and whereas he'd spend approximately the requisite half-an-hour with many students he'd spend a little longer with Hammett simply because he enjoyed playing the guitar with him. Hammett had a totally different approach to playing the guitar than Satriani's other students because his influences were intricate European players like Uli Jon Roth and Michael Schenker, both of whom are German.

Hammett confessed in 1996: "Joe was a big influence back then… but not so much these days. He showed me how to use modes, and he showed me a lot of theory – like what chords to play over what scales, and vice versa. I learned a lot of finger exercises, as well. I had lessons from 1983 'till like '87, on and off – maybe four lessons a year, sometimes. I never had enough time 'cause I was always touring! And then when he hit big with *Surfing With The Alien* he didn't have time either. In fact, I think I was probably his last student."[lx]

The former Exodus guitarist also shared several similar musical influences with the members of Metallica. He enthused: "We've toured with a lot of these bands, and a lot are inspirations… Like Judas Priest, huge inspiration… Lynyrd Skynyrd is a huge inspiration, Mercyful Fate is a huge inspiration…"[lxi]

Hammett first met Ulrich and Hetfield during his tenure in Metallica and liked them both, especially Hetfield as they both played the guitar and had similar backgrounds and influences. It took Hammett some time to warm to Ulrich's idiosyncratic

European traits. "The first time I spoke to him was when Exodus played with Metallica," Hammett informed Jaan Uhelszki. "They had just finished their set and as I was talking to him, he started taking his stage clothes off, and before I knew it he was completely naked in front of me. I was just shocked."[lxii]

In May, 1983, Metallica with their new guitarist Kirk Hammett – who had barely been in the band a month – ventured to Music America in Rochester, New York to begin work on their debut album which was to be called *Metal Up Your Ass*. Hammett learned Mustaine's chords surprisingly quickly and given the short amount of time he had to get used to Metallica's music he did a superlative job. With every show he got better and better and though he wasn't keen on playing Mustaine's solos he didn't want to cause any contention within the band; after all he was the newbie. He sometimes adapted the solos by using the first four bars of Mustaine's solos and then changing them. The band liked what he did.

The recording sessions for the first album lasted between May 10 and 27. Obviously Dave Mustaine wasn't too pleased to hear about Kirk Hammett. Clearly still smarting from recent events, in 1984 he told metal writer and fan Bob Nalbandian: "Kirk is a 'Yes' man..." He went on to say, "It shows you they're having a lot of trouble with this 'New Guitar God!'"[lxiii] However, it's important to note that this quote was made long before Mustaine would make friends with Hetfield, Hammett and Ulrich and truly put the past behind him; his band Megadeth would even appear on stage with Metallica in the future, such as at the Fillmore in San Francisco at the last 30th Anniversary Show on December 10, 2011. Both bands are now firmly established as legends in the metal genre.

What was the relationship like between the four of them – drummer Lars Ulrich, bassist Cliff Burton and guitarists James Hetfield and Kirk Hammett? Bands are complicated creations. A solo artist can have full control over his or her work with only the record label to fight against and that can be a troublesome experience alone, but a band has each other to argue with as well as the label and everything else that comes with the complicated process of making and distributing music. "It's really difficult because I think increasingly as I get older, I'm becoming more and more aware of what the word luck plays into it," drummer Ulrich explained years later as a much older, more experienced man. "I would say that the most important thing in the long run is being with people you can communicate with and that even if you don't share the same vision, you can communicate about the different things. If it's a group thing you have to show other people the same respect that you want them to show you."[lxiv]

"Lars Ulrich had a plan!," says photographer Bill Hale. "And that was to make Metallica the biggest band on the planet! Lars knew what he wanted, who he wanted to work with and how to get it."[lxv]

Ulrich had come to appreciate the way Iron Maiden had been managed by Rod Smallwood; the merchandise they created, the way they co-operated with fans, the care they had over their music and promotion and so on. It all helped Maiden become the biggest metal band in the world in the early-to-mid-1980s. That kind of focus and the long-term planning was a big inspiration to Ulrich who was sitting on the sidelines watching Maiden's world domination come to fruition. Of course, it was primarily about music but to be as big as Maiden meant creating a business; a brand name that would last for generations. Ulrich had his own plans and took inspiration from other bands and eventually manifested them into his own goals. It would take some time but Ulrich knew what he wanted to do.

There is a dual partnership in a band that dominates everything from the way the band performs live on stage to the recording of a song. This duo is the creative force: we've seen it with Lennon and McCartney in The Beatles and Keith Richards and Mick Jagger in the Rolling Stones. The duo is often the singer and the guitarist. With Queen, however, the four of them fought like cats and dogs and the balance of power was almost (though not evenly) balanced between them all. Kirk Hammett later confessed to *Rolling Stone*: "It was evident that it was Lars's and James' band. We still made major decisions together. But whenever I had to push for an idea, I had to assume the role of diplomat. I had to sell them the idea."[lxvi]

Metallica soaked up their influences ranging from the New Wave Of British Heavy Metal bands like Diamond Head and Saxon as well as bands that appealed to punk and metal fans such as Iron Maiden (Paul Di'Anno era) and Motörhead and not forgetting Misfits, Ramones and Black Flag. Those bands displayed a brutal mix of metal and hardcore punk and it was that hybrid sound that Metallica wanted to create on their debut. Ulrich in particular loved the brutality of the hardcore punk bands and wanted to incorporate that style into Metallica's music but they were still a metal band through and through. It was the punk attitude and ethos that appealed to him. Brian Slagel says, "In their early gigs they mostly played Diamond Head and Blitzkrieg covers. They certainly sounded more European than most bands. They also had a bit of a punk element too that helped set them apart."[lxvii]

Though Mustaine was no longer in the band his contributions to the album were still valid: four of the Metallica's songs feature co-writing credits from Mustaine. 'The Four Horsemen', which was originally titled 'The Mechanix', is probably the most notable example. It was an early staple in Metallica's set-list although after Mustaine's departure the band added a melodic middle-section that differed from Mustaine's original, faster tempo version. 'Phantom Lord' and 'Metal Militia' were Mustaine's other songwriting contributions. As with 'The Four Horsemen', the lyrics for 'Jump In The Fire' were reworked by Hetfield though Mustaine kept a co-credit. Hetfield is solely credited with having penned 'Motorbreath' and Burton for the bass solo '(Anesthesia) Pulling Teeth'. Many of the songs had already been created in one way or another prior to the recording of *Kill 'Em All.*

Hetfield: "They [lyrics] were where our heads were at, so they were absolutely right because that was how we felt. And I wouldn't change anything about them. Just the honesty and the innocence of it all is so cool. It's all we knew at the time..."[lxviii]

Perhaps Hetfield wasn't the most sophisticated lyricist at that point but he knew what he wanted to say and learned a lot from the punk bands. Lyrically he could relate to the Pistols and the

Ramones more than he could to Priest and Maiden. However, it is a misconception that the aforementioned British heavy metal bands wrote exclusively about fantasy-style imagery set in imaginative lands. Priest's 'Running Wild' for example is a song about misspent youth and adolescent angst while Maiden (with singer Paul Di'Anno) certainly looked and sounded like a punk band straight off the mean streets of inner city London. Similarly Maiden's 'Wrathchild' is about a young man who is looking for his father after finding out his birth was unplanned. For many rockers, the dungeons-and-dragons-type lyrics were too corny yet for others it created a world of heroes and villains. It was all make-believe; it was like a Michael Moorcock fantasy novel come alive in a world of music. Nevertheless, it was something Metallica avoided. From Hetfield's perspective, a song was about creating a lyrical world that any disenchanted kid in America could relate to, thus creating some kind of kinship between the band and their audience. Certainly having Burton in the band shaped the feel and direction of the lyrics because he was well versed in music and had a better education in music history too. Metallica wanted their music and lyrics to be set in the real world.

Interestingly what the band cooked up in the studio was an idea to have many of the songs – notably 'Phantom Lord', 'Hit The Lights' and 'No Remorse' – sound like they had been recorded live with slow build-ups at the beginning and ferocious climaxes. It's that kind of raw, destructive metallic sound that made their earlier recordings so distinctive.

The guitar parts on the album were recorded through James Hetfield's now famous Marshall amp (his first). The famed Marshall had been modified by Jose Arredondo who had also modified Van Halen's sound equipment and it gave this particular amp a fantastic sound. The budget was tight and the band's finances were low. They didn't have techs or roadies and engineers. They didn't walk around with a large entourage and make over the top demands. At that point in their career Metallica was a low-key band. They practically did everything themselves. Hetfield used a white Gibson Flying V and Hammett used a black Gibson Flying V. Hammett also recorded his guitar solos in the control room. One thing Hammett disliked was playing and listening to his guitar parts through headphones whilst recording; his preferred way gave his guitars a live, more raw feel.

There was no question about including 'Hit The Lights' on their debut album. The old Leather Charm song was reworked a few times by the band with different arrangements. As with most bands, Metallica drew inspiration from some of their heroes. For 'Hit The Lights', Metallica wanted a song as powerful as Queen's 'Great King Rat' and 'Stone Cold Crazy', the latter being a song Metallica covered on the two disc album, *Garage Inc.* 'The Four Horsemen', on the other hand, is as catchy and melodic as Lynyrd Skynrd's 'Sweet Home Alabama'. But it was just another case of Metallica soaking up their influences in the studio. Indeed, 'Jump In The Fire' was purportedly influenced by Iron Maiden's 'Run To The Hills' which was a hit during Metallica's time in the studio. 'Seek & Destroy' also reminds the listener of Diamond Head's 'Dead Reckoning' and Saxon's 'Princess Of The Night' in parts.

Cliff Burton was certainly a powerful and dominant force in the studio which is not often the case with bassists. Burton cemented his musical stamp during 'The Four Horsemen' and even his vocals can be heard during the bridge section. He certainly brought a more technical aspect into the band's camp. Burton was full of ideas and creativity and the rest of the band were impressed by his tireless energy and new ideas.

The minimal production effects gave the album a rawness and aggression with sleeve credits citing Paul Curcio onboard as producer; also Curcio as executive producer and Chris Bubacz engineer with Alex Perialas (spelt 'Perialis' on the original LP pressing) down as mastering engineer. The speed, intensity and raw aggression came from a band that was also nervous; they were young and inexperienced. However, the band had a clear vision of what they wanted to do and despite a low budget they gave it their best shot. (George Marino, who is a well-known name in rock and metal circles, would master later reissues of the album.)

Still young and relatively inexperienced in the studio, Ulrich was nevertheless rather quick to voice his opinion about Metallica's experience of capturing that first album; the band felt isolated from the recording process at times and he later said, 'There's a lot of things that we are really dissatisfied with on the way the album sounds."[lxix]

Just as Saxon had trouble with their original name of Son Of A Bitch, Metallica had disagreements with their label and distributors over the album title *Metal Up Your Ass*. They got a call from the label telling them they had to change the name. Consequently, because of the fuss surrounding the word 'ass' in the title, Metallica changed the album's name to *Kill 'Em All*. As with rap and hip-hop music in the noughties, heavy metal was the cause of many attacks and rebuttals from conservative voters and right-wing fundamentalists throughout the 1980s so record companies were often cautious about censorship fearing it would damage sales and give bad publicity. The name of Metallica's debut came from something Cliff Burton said after hearing that the label and management objected to *Metal Up Your Ass*. Kirk Hammett recalled: "Cliff said, 'You know what? Fuck those fuckers, man, those fucking record outlet people. We should just kill 'em all... Someone, I can't remember who, said, 'That's it! That's what we should call the album.'"[lxx]

Indeed, the album title was not the only problem the band's label took a well-known issue to; they also took objection to the original album cover. Just as self-proclaimed Metal gods Judas Priest had problems with the artwork for *British Steel* (their 1980 classic which has a razor blade on the cover), Metallica's original idea for the *Kill 'Em All* artwork was a hand emerging from a toilet with a dagger, like some cheesy B-movie horror from the 1940s (a special area of interest for Kirk Hammett who collects horror memorabilia and comics). The band were told by their management to use photographer Gary L. Heard to shoot the back cover band shot but he also wanted direct ideas for the front cover artwork from the band too. "Cliff Burton mentioned something about wanting there to be a bloody hammer on the cover – but then Cliff carried a hammer with him everywhere

he went," Hammett told writer Jaan Uhelszki for *musicradar.com*. "He always had a hammer in his luggage, and he would take it out occasionally and start destroying things!"[lxxi] Cliff's main reason for carrying the hammer was that "You never know when you might need it."

The officially released album cover features the shadow of a hand letting go of a hammer with blood dripping from it (the band later released official T-shirts with the original album cover and title *Metal Up Your Ass*. A live bootleg from 1982 is also in existence with the original title and album artwork). It was in many ways the personification of a rebellious band. "When Metallica started we were the outlaws, the rebels," Kirk Hammett admitted. "No one wanted to have anything to do with us. We were too harsh and thought of as the lowliest of the low. All those beginning years we thought we were never getting anywhere or making an impact. Then one day we woke up and it was like, 'Oh my God – we're famous; everyone knows us.'"[lxxii]

Kill 'Em All opens with the furious 'Hit The Lights'. It's a fantastic thrash metal song that harks back to the aggression of Motörhead's classic track 'Overkill' and the in-your-face attitude of punk bands like the Sex Pistols. The musicianship is robust with some powerful drumming and excellent riffing courtesy of Hetfield and Hammett; the central guitar solo by Hammett is a real killer. This is the kind of song that Metallica excelled at in the earlier part of their career. Lyrically 'Hit The Lights' is about life on the road, playing in a metal band and performing in front of an audience. 'The Four Horsemen' – an apt title for the four member band – has become a fan favourite over the years. There's a middle melodic section which has a fairly distinctive and well-structured guitar solo and Hetfield's voice throughout the song is typically angry. The lyrics are about the end of the world; the apocalypse. In the Bible, there is text about The Four Horsemen Of The Apocalypse: Time, Famine, Pestilence and Death. In past texts, the Biblical interpretations were Conquest, War, Famine and Death. Metal bands have always been fascinated by religion and various religious rites and ceremonies and this is either represented in their lyrics or the artwork (or both). 'The Four Horsemen Of The Apocalypse' is a consistently powerful song with enormous fan appeal.

Next up is 'Motorbreath', which is an obvious homage to one of Metallica's favourite bands. The three-minute track is as fast as any Ramones song and as angry as any killer Motörhead tune. As with 'Hit The Lights', there is a drum intro by Ulrich before the guitars kick in. For many fans, this is what metal is about: there's plenty of scope to headbang and the drums are as powerful as anything Ulrich does on this opus. Lyrically, 'Motorbreath' is about living live to the full, no regrets and no remorse, enjoying life to the limits and so forth. This song is the only one that is credited to Hetfield alone while only one of two (the other being the Burton-penned track '(Anesthesia) Pulling Teeth') where Ulrich does not have a songwriting credit. 'Jump In The Fire' has an interesting history like many of the tracks on *Kill 'Em All*. Lyrically, Dave Mustaine's original words were basically about sex but were later reworked by Hetfield and the lyrics on *Kill 'Em All* came from Satan's point of view as he watches people murdering one another, thus making sure they will go to hell for their hideous acts (i.e. they will jump in the fire). It's a devil of a song – excuse the pun – with a fantastic, almost progressive, riff. Typically, it is an angry track but it has one of the album's standout choruses.

Here's a track that doesn't often appear on an album: '(Anesthesia) Pulling Teeth' is just a bass solo but a bass solo like no other. It's a thumping, remarkable track with heavy distortion and Burton's distinctive use of wah-wah pedal and tapping. Like Motörhead's mainman Lemmy, Burton played his bass like a lead guitar and consequently it made the tracks on this album all the more distinctive. It's a surprisingly melodic track too; about two minutes in the bass speeds up as Lars Ulrich's drums kick in and the pair jam together. The song leads up to the kick-ass thrash metal beast known as 'Whiplash'. It has one of the most distinctive beginnings of any Metallica song: there's a fantastic lead up to the introduction of the riffs and it has a raw energy and powerful kick to it, which makes it one of Metallica's best songs from any era or album of their career. Lyrically, as the title might suggest in one way, it's certainly not about getting whiplashed from a vehicle accident but from headbanging whilst listening to heavy metal, the sort of neck ache and tired feeling you get from headbanging at a metal gig or even at home listening to an album. The guitar interplay between Hetfield and Hammett is top-notch.

Named after one of James Hetfield's former bands, 'Phantom Lord' is basically about mythical beasts battling each other. It doesn't sound as raw as its *Kill 'Em All* siblings because it was the first time Metallica had given their guitars a more clean, melodic sound in their structure. Perhaps it's one of the albums least well-known or referred to tracks but that doesn't stop it from having its merits; there's a brilliant guitar solo in the middle and there's also a brief melodic interlude part way through that proves Metallica were certainly not a one dimensional thrash metal outfit. 'No Remorse' is a superlative Metallica track with rapid changes in tempo and guitar riffs; it sounds like an angry, thirsty young metal band wanting to take on the world which was exactly what Metallica were attempting to do at that stage in their career. On the lyrics front, 'No Remorse' is basically about people not feeling any remorse or repent or sorrow during war. It's the perfect song to represent Metallica at the very beginning of their career. 'Seek & Destroy' remains one of the most well known Metallica songs of all time and has been played at almost every single live performance they have ever done. It's a great live song with a chorus that's perfect for the band to get their fans to sing-along to. It opens with some melodic guitars before the drums smoothly kick in and then all hell breaks loose. As is often the case, subsequent live versions have been much faster and heavier than the original studio version but it remains a monster of a song. Three minutes into the track there's an instrumental section that begins with Ulrich's drums before the guitars interrupt and accompany the drumming. 'Seek & Destroy' remains a force to be reckoned with in Metallica's now extensive back catalogue. The album closes with 'Metal Militia', probably Metallica's fastest song. It's a superb track about the band as the Metal Militia taking on the rest of the world with their metal, spreading their message. It's the perfect way to end the album.

Overall, *Kill 'Em All* is an awesome low-budget metal album and it is easy to see why it has become one of metal's most iconic pieces of work. It also represents a time in Metallica's career when they were young and hungry for recognition which is why they could never release this kind of album again. There is a feeling in

Attention Metallibangers:

We at the Stateside branch of the **METALLICA METAL MILITIA** apologize for the lengthy delay in reply due to circumstances beyond our control. Despite pitfalls and setbacks, however, we are now in full operation and eager to recruit and unite all dedicated Metallibangers nationwide in a quest to promote and encourage America's premier practitioners of audio death, **METALLICA!** In cooperation with Megaforce Records and manager John Zazula, we've combined forces to "bang that head that doesn't bang" whilst spreading the word about the band. At the same time, we're offering a wide array of merchandise ala shirts, buttons, and upcoming items which will soon be available to headbanging hordes nationwide.

Join the **METALLICA METAL MILITIA** and receive:

Quarterly Newsletter
Merchandising Info
Glossy Photo (Autographed for 1st 100 applicants)
Future benefits of MM Membership

Send membership fee of $5.00 (check or money order) to: **Metal Militia**, 345 W. Riverside Dr., Roseburg, OR 97470. Please allow 6-8 weeks for delivery. In the meantime . . . M.U.Y.A.!!!

Yours Metallically,
K. J. Doughton
Metal Militia President

some circles however, that Metallica were merely mimicking their idols and that they needed to develop their own style rather more. What it may lack in originality, the album more than makes up for with high doses of energy and stamina.

As a piece of heavy metal history it speaks volumes, quite literally. *Kill 'Em All* remains a totally brutal and destructive metal album. It is undoubtedly one of the key albums in the thrash metal scene. It was at this point that American metal was on the rise though it would take a few more years for Metallica's profile to go global. Nevertheless, kudos to Messrs Lars Ulrich, James Hetfield, Cliff Burton and Kirk Hammett.

Metallica's debut album was released via Megaforce Records in the States in June 1983 and through Music For Nations in Europe the following month. It eventually peaked at Number 155 in the *Billboard* 200 album charts in 1986 but did not chart initially. When it was released by Elektra in 1988 it peaked at Number 120 (in the UK it did not chart either on its initial release). Though the album was not a great commercial success it did increase the band's fanbase and cement their new line-up: drummer Lars Ulrich, guitarists James Hetfield and Kirk Hammett and bassist Cliff Burton. Their debut album spawned the singles 'Whiplash', 'Jump In The Fire' and 'Seek & Destroy'. All classics in their own right although it must be pointed out here that 'Whiplash' actually won Motörhead their first and so far only Grammy Award for 'Best Metal Performance' in 2005 from the Metallica tribute album, *Metallic Attack: The Ultimate Tribute*. It was especially ironic because Metallica were – and still are – hugely influenced by Motörhead so for the British band to win a Grammy for covering one of Metallica's songs was an odd turnaround of events but it certainly helped raise Motörhead's global profile.

"This release pretty much set the whole speed/thrash metal ball rolling, and for that reason alone *Kill 'Em All* is a crucial album," comments *Metal Forces'* Bernard Doe. "There was already a huge buzz surrounding the band thanks to the tape trading scene, and *Kill 'Em All* was also probably the most anticipated debut release ever from an underground metal band. Of course,

Metallica would go on to write better material, but even now it's still a great album and to me 'Whiplash' remains an anthem that epitomises that whole era."[lxxiii]

Despite having released an album, the band were still broke. Kirk Hammett: "We were living very, very meagerly. The only time I had money was when we went out on the road and had *per diems* [on tour daily allowances]. I remember on our first tour, we got ten bucks a day on days off and seven bucks on a show day because we could always eat free at the gig."[lxxiv]

Critical opinion was perhaps not as widespread as the band would have hoped but it was an underground metal album after all. *Kill 'Em All* didn't exactly set the world alight nor did it make *Kerrang!*'s famed end of year poll list which for 1983 included Def Leppard at Number 1 with *Pyromania* and other artists including KISS (*Lick It Up*), Journey (*Frontiers*) and Dio (*Holy Diver*). Luckily for the band, from a UK perspective at the time of the release *of Kill 'Em All,* a magazine in the vein of Ron Quintana's *Metal Mania* had been created in the UK as a sort of response to the more commercial music that *Kerrang!* was covering. *Metal Forces* aimed to expose young up-and-coming metal bands as well as the underground metal scene.

Metal Forces co-founder and editor Bernard Doe reflects, "I was already a big Metallica fan before *Metal Forces* was launched, having been sent their demos during my tape trading days in 1982. In fact, I was officially selling Metallica tapes for the band in the UK through Shades [a now legendary but sadly defunct London record store] prior to the release of *Kill 'Em All*. So, I was particularly proud to have been the first UK journalist to interview Metallica and put the band on the cover of our third issue... *Metal Forces* was never a thrash magazine, but we were certainly at the forefront of the thrash explosion and our coverage of the genre was second to none during the 1980s."[lxxv]

Indeed, Doe saw the potential in the band and raved about their debut release in issue one of *Metal Forces*. He enthused: "The debut album by Metallica has been a long time coming, but it's definitely been worth waiting for as it's a real killer! Certainly not for the faint hearted, each track is guaranteed for 100% brain destruction!!!" Doe continued: "Metallica deliver their metal with such power, speed and precision that they make a lot of other so-called heavy metal bands seem tame and feeble."

Bob Nalbandian wrote in his *Headbanger* fanzine: "*Kill 'Em All* displays OTT, ultra-fast, riff-orientated metal... And to think that I had doubts when drummer Lars Ulrich once told me a couple of years ago that he was gonna form the heaviest metal band in the US! Anyhow, *Kill 'Em All* delivers 100% Power Metal, not advised to be purchased by those with weak hearts."

On future reissues, publications would rave over the album. Here's what the rock and metal scribes said in the noughties. *Rolling Stone*: "It contains the first great Metallica standard, 'Seek & Destroy', not to mention the instrumental '(Anesthesia) Pulling Teeth', which features the late Cliff Burton delivering the greatest metal bass solo ever, for what it's worth. But the remainder of the album reflects the cover photo of four zitty teenagers trying to look tough."

Punks News declared: "The guitars are the highlight of this album. All the main riffs are memorable and even a lot of the secondary ones are as well. Kirk Hammett's lead work is frantic (no pun) and energetic, and several of the solos on this album rank among his best ... Every song on this album is unique and contributes something to the album in total."

Metal Storm enthused: "The history of the best metal band began with this CD. In this album the bases of thrash metal appeared for first time. By this time Metallica was surely the fastest band in the world, even faster than Venom [precursors of black metal style]. In this CD Metallica finds its own style which some years later will bring them to the top of metal."

Metal Observer was very impressed: "That time, they had the Hetfield/Ulrich/Mustaine and Burton line-up and the young band from the Bay Area created a true speed/thrash metal highlight. Raw, fast and crude, the band thrashes through true speed metal shells like 'Whiplash', 'Motorbreath' or 'Phantomlord' [*sic*]. Though the sound isn't as pressuring as on later releases, you can still listen to it harmlessly today. Maybe, it's because of this sound, that mangily [filthy/raw sound], that spirit of *Kill 'Em All*, which makes this album so irresistible. Every guitar solo, every punch on the drums is in the right place."

Steve Huey of *All Music* stated: "The true birth of thrash. On *Kill 'Em All*, Metallica fuses the intricate riffing of New Wave Of British Heavy Metal bands like Judas Priest, Iron Maiden, and Diamond Head with the velocity of Motörhead and hardcore punk… Frightening, awe-inspiring, and absolutely relentless, *Kill 'Em All* is pure destructive power, executed with jaw-dropping levels of scientific precision."

Suite101 expressed keenness for the album and its historical appeal: "*Kill 'Em All* was a great catalyst for Metallica. They were also playing live shows, building their reputation and gaining followers with their type of music. With the record, they were testing the waters for recognition. With the technical structuring of the songs outdoing the lyrics by quite a margin, Metallica still had a long way to go in being an accomplished, polished band. As a debut album, it didn't quite set the world on fire, but instead stirred and created interest. The world would follow soon after."

The Canadian metal historian and author Martin Popoff examines the album's strengths and weaknesses as he told the author of this book: "My impressions upon hearing *Kill 'Em All* for the first time haven't really changed much. There was always one thing that kept it from being an absolute masterpiece, and that's this idea that it seems to be an album that is all about riff and very little else. It's almost like all other performances gather around and marvel at these amazing riffs, and they are amazing, but really every song seemed to be built and focused purely on riff. Part of this has to do with the production. It's a good, fierce production job, but there is a separation that also makes you compartmentalise, simplify, focus on rhythm guitar, with everybody else just supporting. Even James – when it comes to the vocals, it sounds like they are there to react to and support the riff as well, to egg on the riffs. Still, there was something new and nasty about the record. Obviously, almost all of the important NWOBHM albums had come and gone, and this seemed to be a band that was netting out the pure bleached heaviness from all of that and focusing purely on that, providing the Coles notes, the greatest hits of the NWOBHM. That's what I took away from that album and still take away from that album, a fierceness and nastiness, an even greater understanding of heavy metal that began with the NWOBHM, those British bands being the first that sort of put the message out there that we could be proud of metal."[lxxvi]

Evidently, the legacy of *Kill 'Em All* is assured; there is no question about that. It has sold three million copies in the United States alone and had been certified Platinum three times by 1999. It sold around 300,000 copies upon its original release but sales quickly picked up half-a-million by 1989 and progressed thereafter. In 1989 *Kerrang!* proclaimed it to be one of the '100 Greatest Metal Albums Of All Time' (Number 29, specifically) and in 1998 *Kerrang!* also said it was one of the '100 Albums You Must Hear Before You Die' (specifically at Number 83). It is certainly hailed as one of metal's finest achievements and regularly crops up in various album polls related to the thrash era or metal in general (sometimes even popular music as a whole). For example, in 1989, *Rolling Stone* magazine rated it Number 35 in 'The 100 Greatest Albums Of The 1980s'. *Hit Parader* proclaimed it the Number 1 'Underground Album' and *Metal-Rules.com* had it down as the twentieth album in their 'Best Metal Albums Ever' poll.

Despite the blatant influence Diamond Head and their NWOBHM ilk had on Metallica and *Kill 'Em All,* the album slipped off Brian Tatler's radar for quite some time. He explained to the author, "I did not hear *Kill 'Em All* till about 2005. Lars had sent me several Metallica albums over the years including *Puppets, Justice* and *The Black Album* [*Metallica*] but I never had the first album. James's vocal style owes a debt to Sean Harris on that record and it reminds me of Diamond Head in places but having said that, it is uniquely their own."[lxxvii]

Tatler continued: "I am constantly amazed at their incredible success and their longevity. If I had heard *Kill 'Em All* in 1983 I would not have put money on them becoming the biggest metal band of all time, who would? They have worked extremely hard for it though; this kind of success is not easily achieved."[lxxviii]

In September, 2007, Dave Grohl of the Foo Fighters confessed to *Kerrang!*: "I still listen to *Kill 'Em All* once a week and there's a part of me that will never lose the love of riffs. That's where a song like this comes in. As a drummer and a guitar player, the rhythmic quality of a decent riff is like a cannon to me. I can write riffs all day long because I look at the guitar like a drum set. So, just as I'll sit at a drum kit and play beats, I sit with a guitar and try the same thing."[lxxix]

Anthrax's Scott Ian has rated it as one of his Top 10 thrash metal albums of all time alongside Slayer's *Reign In Blood*, Suicidal Tendencies self-titled opus, Exodus' *Bonded By Blood*, Venom's *Welcome To Hell*, Raven's *Rock Until You Drop*, Anvil's *Metal On Metal*, Mercyful Fate's self-titled EP, Pantera's *Vulgar Display Of Power* and Megadeth's *Killing Is My Business... And Business Is Good!*. He said: "We were listening to them so much back at that time, and I couldn't listen to that more than I was back then when it first came out. That EP (sic) was a huge influence on everything that was to come. The playing, riff-wise, that thrash element is certainly there in the guitars."[lxxx]

The reverence that has been bestowed upon Metallica's debut album has not diminished over the years; in fact it has grown stronger and it is the kind of raw and aggressive album that some fans would like to see Metallica releasing in the 21st Century. Though it may have only made a minor splash on its original release, as Metallica's profile evolved to enormous God-like heights in the late 1980s and thereafter, the album's popularity also rose considerably.

Metallica began their first ever tour – the '*Kill 'Em All* For One Tour' – on July 27, 1983, which would run for dozens of shows until September 3 with the NWOBHM band Raven. James Hetfield said: "There were really horrible smells on that bus as there was a lot of drinking, puking and fucking going on. You would have to get drunk to actually fall asleep on that thing as it was so horrible. We would always fight for the top bunk. The air conditioner broke down somewhere in Texas, so it was about 200 degrees when you woke up!"[lxxxi]

The tour was financed by Megaforce while the band's set-list mostly consisted of songs from their upcoming debut and leftover material that would later be used on their second studio release. Their regular set-list ran as follows: 'Hit The Lights', 'The Four Horsemen', 'Jump In The Fire', 'Fight Fire With Fire', 'Ride The Lightning', 'Phantom Lord', 'The Call Of Ktulu', 'No Remorse', 'Seek & Destroy', '(Anesthesia) Pulling Teeth', 'Whiplash', 'Creeping Death' and 'Metal Militia'.

James Hetfield: "That was where we cut our teeth on the road. We actually got to do one show with Motörhead, Raven and us. Getting out there playing fields in the middle of Arkansas to your dumpy little club called the Rat in Chicago was great. We made a lot of friends on that tour. It was also pretty amazing to find out how our demo tape had gotten across the country and taken a hold on a lot of the young, angry youth of America."[lxxxii]

By this point, Metallica were building up a reputation as a powerful live act. They continued to play some cover versions and alternate the selection of other artists' songs with each gig but they also played a significant amount of their own material. They were faithful to the original songs. "I think a lot of that, particularly with the older covers, was because we really didn't know that we had our own style," Hetfield admitted. "We were inspired by those songs, so we played them like the original versions."[lxxxiii] Metallica never did shy away from paying tributes to their heroes and they had fun doing it.

They were becoming tauter, leaner and better rehearsed with each gig. Cliff Burton said in February, 1986: "Different shows have different good points and it's really great to do a big show in front of the home town. But there's also other gigs, like when things are really, really happening. There's been a few of those. There's different things that make different shows memorable. I couldn't pinpoint one as being my favourite."[lxxxiv]

After initially wanting to have someone else as a frontman, James Hetfield was coming out of his shell gig after gig and transforming himself into a powerful onstage force. He was learning how to talk to a crowd, how to control them and how to get them to work with the music. Initially, he didn't sing and play at the same time but he was soon doing both tasks, and in time he became a natural.

Over a decade later, James Hetfield confessed: "Maybe some of that singing/playing thing started when I was forced to take piano lessons as a kid. Doing the two-hand thing gets your brain thinking a couple different things at once. In the early days, singing was just something that I had to do, because I couldn't let all those lame guys sing for us. I'm gonna do it. But then that guy's not playing the riff right – give me the guitar back!"[lxxxv]

He continued: "It was a battle for which thing I wanted to do.

CERTIFICATE OF MEMBERSHIP
This Certifies That
METALLICA METALLICA
Is A Member of Metallica's Metal Militia And Is Entitled To All Rights And Privileges Thereof
Membership Valid Through ____________
President

People would say, 'Your band's not going to do shit unless you have a frontman. You've got to have a singer out there who's got his hands free to do stuff,' to throw the fucking sign or whatever."[lxxxvi]

Metallica had a little bit more material to play onstage than the previous year but they still covered other bands' songs; however it was becoming easier for them to play a full set of originals. "Like any other band starting out, we would cover material because we needed to have enough songs to fill up the set when we played live," Hetfield said. "We had 'Hit The Lights', 'The Four Horsemen' and a few others, but not enough originals to do a full set. And since we were covering songs by these British heavy metal bands, people thought they were our own songs."[lxxxvii]

In October, the band announced the demo tapes for *Ride The Lightning* which would wet the lips of metal fans who were eagerly awaiting their second studio album. They also spent time on tour from October to December. However, just before they commenced recording of the aforementioned demos for their second studio opus, they hit problems after a reported £40,000 worth of equipment was stolen from the band at a hotel in Boston just a week before a tour with Anthrax commenced. After the theft, a cautious Lars Ulrich then flew to London earlier than scheduled to arrange the hiring of new gear. Hetfield's precious Marshall amp head was taken and it took some time for him to find a replacement that had the right Metallica sound. For the remaining three shows on the tour, Anthrax kindly loaned Metallica their stage gear. This prompted Metallica to write a song called 'Fade To Black'.

Fans were waiting for something fresh from Metallica; something mind-blowing. *Kill 'Em All* was only a taste of things to come…

Ride The Lightning
1984

"We're like a gang. They have their jobs, we have our jobs. Our jobs don't start until 7:30 or so, so we just wait around, skate..."

Kirk Hammett[lxxxviii]

Metallica's peers included many bands in the north California area which became known as the Bay Area thrash scene, groups such as Exodus, Testament, Sadus and Possessed. There were also thrash metal outfits in southern California such as Slayer and Dave Mustaine's new outfit, Megadeth. This led to the rise of American thrash and death metal. Meanwhile, the New York thrash outfit Anthrax had formed in 1981 and released their killer debut *Fistful Of Metal* in 1984 and were leaders of the East Coast thrash metal scene along with the New Jersey band Overkill.

Thrash wasn't specifically restricted to America although it may have seemed that way: the German thrash trio Sodom had formed in 1981 while Destruction and Kreator both formed in 1982. They were the pioneers of European technical thrash and death metal and became known as 'the three kings' of Teutonic thrash metal. Suffice it to say there were regional thrash metal scenes all over the world but it was spearheaded primarily by American and German bands. Later, Brazil evolved a growing metal scene led by the band Stress and Canada spawned Anvil, Exciter, Voivod and later in the decade, Annihilator. Many of these bands stayed on a cult level without the mass appeal that would be given to Metallica. Jeff Waters of Annihilator told the author: "When I was younger I had dreams of being [in] Metallica; just as a kid you dream about getting to this level and over the years you get slapped down to reality and you realise you should be happy where you are."[lxxxix]

This isn't a book to debate the difference between speed metal and thrash metal but suffice it to say thrash evolved from speed metal. A band liked Anvil and Exciter (both from Canada) have been dubbed speed while Metallica are thrash. Exciter's John Ricci told the author, "Speed metal is closer in style to power metal which is like big power chords played fast with melodic vocals; thrash is more like a guitar riff with a whole bunch of notes crammed in a very short space in the music therefore you can't really distinguish the riff and once this fast riffing is combined with lots of distortion you have thrash."[xc]

It is important to know the difference between thrash and speed and what makes Metallica a thrash band. Speed metal evolved from such songs as 'Communication Breakdown' by Led Zeppelin, 'Highway Star' and 'Fireball' by Deep Purple, 'Sheer Heart Attack' and 'Stone Cold Crazy' by Queen and much of Motörhead's back catalogue, including 'Bomber' and 'Overkill'.

David Konow – author of *Bang Your Head: The Rise And Fall Of Heavy Metal* – spoke to the author about the difference between speed metal and thrash and what specifically pigeon-holed Metallica in the latter subgenre of metal. He states: "I always found the subgenre labels of metal, like many found them, to be a bit confusing and head scratching, especially these days with screamo, this, that, whatever... It was never properly defined to me in all my years as a metalhead. Speed metal was supposed to be mostly fast, thrash had slower 'mosh' parts, and things like that is how I vaguely remember it being once defined. Metallica always strove very hard to leave all that stuff behind and not be pigeonholed into that category. It's a big reason I always liked their music, it had more to it than Venom and Slayer, who I loved as well, but their style was more one-dimensional. Metallica had more variety to what they were doing, they were really good musicians too, and it's also what I loved about Megadeth's first two albums, the musicianship was up to a much higher standard and they were more experimental with what they were doing. Although they always knew they'd get cries of 'sell out', Metallica were smart to expand their sound early and not get stuck in one thing, where a lot of bands painted themselves in a corner with their style and couldn't expand on what they were doing. But getting back to the original question, I think with say death metal it's obvious what the difference is, and what defines that sound, and even back in the 1980s there were all these category names like speedcore; grindcore was probably defined around 1987, etc. I still dig a lot of it, and I guess the all-purpose term these days is extreme metal, which a lot of this stuff fits under just fine."[xci]

The American thrash metal scene that was located on both ends of California, the East Coast and also south Florida was the complete opposite to the LA hair metal scene. The LA area in the early 1980s was dominated by glam rock and hair metal bands led by the likes of Mötley Crüe, Poison, Quiet Riot, Dokken, Ratt, W.A.S.P. and Stryper. There were lots of others bands too but the aforementioned ones were some of the more popular and commercially successful outfits. "They [Metallica] were certainly different from anything going on in LA at the time or really in the USA as they were so influenced by the New Wave Of British Heavy metal and European style metal," says Brian Slagel."[xcii]

The glam and hair metal scene wasn't specifically centered around the Sunset Strip as Black 'N Blue came from Oregon, Bon Jovi came from New Jersey and Twisted Sister hailed from Long Island. However, Metallica and their ilk had deliberately distanced themselves from the LA hair metal scene. For them, metal was more technical and intricate and certainly not focused on fashion and hairstyles.

Metallica sided with the elder statesmen of American rock like Aerosmith and Montrose but mostly their influences hailed from Europe where it was less about image and fame but more about music and innovation. Ulrich and Hetfield were also fans of progressive rock, notably the Canadian masters Rush fronted by bassist Geddy Lee. The sense of musicality and innovation that bands like Rush brought to their music was what Metallica wanted to do on their next album; their second full-length opus. It was almost as if prog rock bands sweated over every chord and every verse, such was the indulgent nature of the music. Even though they were now recording their own original material, Metallica still loved to listen to their idols as well as up-and-coming bands.

METALLICA

Metallica, particularly bassist Cliff Burton, was interested in the heavier end of prog rock and Rush was one of those bands. Formed in 1968 in Toronto, Rush began as a blues-tinted heavy metal band inspired by British Invasion bands like The Who, The Kinks and Led Zeppelin et al before they fully embraced progressive rock and began incorporating synthesizers in their music. 1976's masterful opus *2112* was the band's breakthrough album after three previous releases. What Metallica loved about Rush was their sense of musicality, their originality and the melting pot of ideas and styles that was totally unique.

Jon Collins, author of the excellent biography *Rush: Chemistry* says, "In some way thrash metal was an evolution of the more hair metal oriented bands; in some ways, it was a reaction to them and a return to more of the energy levels of the 1970s. I would imagine that Metallica musicians would undoubtedly have been influenced by the virtuosity of Rush; I wouldn't be at all surprised if they didn't take influence from that earlier period – up to *2112*. However, [19]80s Rush were the kind of thing that Metallica were reacting to, with their short hair, jackets and shoelace ties!"[xciii]

Meanwhile, the Canadian writer Martin Popoff – author of the authorised Rush book *Contents Under Pressure* – opines: "I think Rush absolutely was a huge influence on anybody trying to craft metal in 1982, 1983. Even though I never amounted to anything as a drummer, I know for sure I lived that exact same experience as lots of guys, my huge drum kit with nine tom-toms, in the attic of a buddy's house, a lonely pursuit, [Rush song] 'Subdivisions' guy, learning all of Neil's [Peart] licks, able to play them all, just not as smoothly. That guy alone was a huge inspiration on all drummers, because he was such a musical drummer, with his tom fills being drum riffs. In fact, the technicality stopped just short of the crazy jazz guys, or even Bill Bruford. And that's what gave kids that magic opportunity, that possibility that if they worked hard enough, they could work their way through these licks which always sounded heroic and epic in the context of the band's weirdly bubbly and joyous hard rock sound (see 'Limelight' or 'The Spirit Of Radio'). Same thing for bass players. Guitar, I really don't know if Rush was really one of these big guitar inspiration bands. Nobody really talks about it, and for good reason. It's almost like the bass and the drums were metal in combative spirit, but Alex [Lifeson, Rush guitarist] wasn't particularly metal all that often. Anyway, Rush was absolutely the instruction book for many bands. Not to get carried away here, it's not like all of these metal bands only listened to Rush. But Rush was a big part of that woodshedding, learning your instrument thing. And looking specifically at Metallica, sure, large swathes of the band's second, third and fourth albums are progressive metal, and who invented progressive metal, almost single-handedly? Rush. You can even hear Rush in Cliff Burton's bass sound, that buzzy bass, which I guess also, when a bass player wants to be heard, there's inspiration from Geddy, from Lemmy, from Steve Harris. And as an extension, you can hear the influence of Geddy in the fact that there are recurring prominent roles for the bassist in Metallica."[xciv]

Indeed, Burton in particular loved the way prog rock bands like Rush in Canada and Jethro Tull and ELP in England introduced classical influences in their music as well as blues and folk. Ever since he was a teenager in Denmark, Ulrich has also loved rock and metal and their many subgenres.

Metallica had now begun work on their second opus. They wrote the album at a house over in El Cerrito where they'd lived for some time, as Ulrich explained: "It was the refuge, the sanctuary for everybody in the neighbourhood. People would come over and live there, hang there. It was a lot of fun – when you're nineteen."[xcv]

Ride The Lightning was recorded between February 20 and March 14 at Sweet Silence Studios in Copenhagen, Denmark where the British hard rock band Rainbow and the Danish metal group Mercyful Fate had recorded, which was a major source of appeal to Metallica. Kirk Hammett was a huge Mercyful Fate fan. He enthused: "Their stuff was so incredibly heavy and progressive for its time. Their guitarists, Hank Shermann and Michael Denner, wrote some of the best riffs of all time. Musically, they

BUTTON
"KILL 'EM ALL"
Album Cover Art
$1.00

BUTTON
"RIDE THE LIGHTING"
Album Cover Art
$1.00

BUTTON
METALLICA
Red Logo on Black Background
$1.00

JACKET SIZE EMBROIDERED
SEW-ON LOGO PATCH
$5.00

ENAMEL BADGE
Red Logo on Gold Pin
$3.00

METALLICA LIVE CONCERT POSTER
2' × 3'
$4.00

(Other Metal Merchandise, Available — Send Self-Address Stamped Envelope For Information)

QUANTITY	CHECK ITEM / CHECK SIZE	PRICE
	T-SHIRTS S M L XL ☐ KILL EM ALL (S M L XL) ☐ METAL MILITIA (S M L XL) ☐ JUMP IN THE FIRE (S M L XL) ☐ M.U.Y.A. T-SHIRT (S M L XL) ☐ RIDE THE LIGHTING (S M L XL)	
	BUTTON ☐ KILL EM ALL ☐ RIDE THE LIGHTING ☐ LOGO	
	☐ LIVE CONCERT POSTER	
	☐ EMBROIDERED PATCH	
	☐ METAL MILITIA MEMBERSHIP	
	☐ ENAMEL BADGE	
	PLEASE ADD 50¢ PER ITEM FOR SHIPPING	
	TOTAL	

PLEASE SEND
CASH, CHECK OR MONEY ORDER
PAYABLE TO:
RON BOUTWELL ENT.

ADDRESS:
METALLICA METAL MILITIA
22225 P.C.H. #4
MALIBU, CA 90265

PLEASE ALLOW 4 WEEKS FOR DELIVERY.
VOID WHERE PROHIBITED
INTERNATIONAL ORDERS
(OUTSIDE NORTH AMERICA ADD $3 FOR SHIPPING/IMPORTING)

(PLEASE PRINT CLEARLY)
NAME ______
ADDRESS ______
CITY ______ STATE ______ ZIP ______
PHONE # ______

came from the same place that we did: old UFO, Iron Maiden, Diamond Head, Motörhead, Judas Priest, Tygers Of Pan Tang. Fate had an incredibly huge influence on us in the early days."[xcvi]

Mercyful Fate was also a major influence on the young Dane Lars Ulrich. The metal band had formed in Copenhagen in 1981 featuring former members of Black Rose and Brats. They released *The Mercyful Fate* EP in 1982 and followed it up with their debut album *Melissa* in 1983. It has become one of the most enduring albums in metal and Mercyful Fate led the way for lots of the bands in the various extreme ends of metal, including death, thrash, speed, progressive, power and black. Their second album *Don't Break The Oath* (1984) is also a stone cold heavy metal classic. Fronted by King Diamond, they were also an incredibly powerful live band and coming from Denmark, Ulrich was especially fond of them. Some of their music was very intricate and progressive but it would be some time before critics would truly appreciate the sheer power and exhilaration of the band's music. They had an enormous impact on the American thrash metal scene and their influence lasts to this day.

Metallica hooked up with producers Flemming Rasmussen and Mark Whitaker for the next record (the eventual sleeve credits state it was 'Produced by Metallica. Assisted by Flemming Rasmussen and Mark Whitaker). The album would produce one of their most famous tracks, 'For Whom The Bell Tolls'. James Hetfield later confessed: "Lars can throw fills in then and we can get the arrangement tightened up. We started using that method on *Ride The Lightning* for the song 'For Whom The Bell Tolls'. It was just these big, fat open chords – I knew I was going to sing over it and I knew what I was going to do, but no one else did. They were going, 'That song's fucking crap – it's just a bunch of chords.' And then when I laid the vocals down they're going, 'Oh, yeah – it makes sense.'"[xcvii]

Lars Ulrich told *Metal Forces'* Bernard Doe: "Yeah, I think we were as happy as we could be. A few of the songs were only written just before we had to do the album, so I think we might have arranged them a little differently if we had had the opportunity to put them down on tape first, and then gone away and listened to them before doing the album."[xcviii]

The revered George Marino remastered the album while the band came up with the album artwork's concept (the sleeve credit reads 'Cover Concept Metallica. Cover Design: AD Artists'). With this album the band wanted more control than on *Kill 'Em All.* They had a clear vision about the sound of the album and the look of the sleeve and they were less willing to compromise. They were becoming a tighter force as the days passed by and they had a collective vision that they wanted to spread around the world so that in time their music would become a major global force.

How did the recording of *Ride The Lightning* compare to *Kill 'Em All*? The band were much more intimately involved this time: "That's why there's such a drastic sonic difference between *Kill 'Em All* and *Ride The Lightning*."[xcix] The recording of *Ride The Lightning* was squeezed in between Metallica's support slot on Venom's 'Seven Dates Of Hell Tour' of Europe which had kicked off on February 3 in Switzerland and finished on August 29 in France.

Mike Exley, a writer for the UK magazine *Metal Forces*, says, "I think, for Metallica, [Venom] was one of the first things that got the guys into thrash. Ulrich always goes on about the effect of NWOBHM – Diamond Head and their ilk. But old pictures of the day tended to show Hetfield with hardcore punk T-shirts and those bullet wristbands (which if you ever tried making them, were a complete no-no) around his arms; but I think it was the spirit of Venom that really came through in Metallica. I think they loved the honesty of it, the English punk sound Venom had. What some people forget is that on that Seven Dates Of Hell Tour, at least in Europe anyway, Metallica were the support band and got a love for crazy European audiences … *Black Metal* for Venom and *Kill 'Em All* for Metallica, are now seen as the quintessential releases of the period and it was an era of real discovery."[c]

Venom was a massive inspiration to not only Metallica but many of the American and European thrash and death metal bands. Venom formed in Newcastle Upon Tyne in the North East of England in 1979. They were influenced by the likes of Black Sabbath, Judas Priest, Alice Cooper, KISS and Deep Purple. Their first two albums – 1981s *Welcome To Hell* and the following year's *Black Metal* – are landmarks of the metal genre and have been cited as a heavy influence on the thrash metal and extreme metal scene. The second album heavily influenced the extreme metal subgenres death and black metal. Their music and imagery featured many satanic references (often cleverly tongue-in-cheek) and the band members each took stage names such as guitarist Jeff Dunn as Mantas, bassist/singer Conrad Lant as

Cronos and drummer Tony Bray as Abaddon. Songs like 'Cold Gin' and 'Black Diamond' are fantastic rock songs and Venom continued to make the kind of metal that fans associated with such theatrical and devilish imagery. They released *At War With Satan* in 1984, which as a record was far more progressive than its predecessors.

Metallica played their first UK gig in the English capital on Tuesday, March 27, 1984. This was a hastily arranged show after the UK tour with The Rods and Exciter was cancelled due to lower than expected ticket sales. The Marquee show was an instant sell-out, so an extra date was added on April 8. Tickets were just £3 and doors opened at 7:30p.m. Original Tygers Of Pang Tang frontman Jess Cox told the author: "'Hi, can you autograph my sticks?' said this little guy backstage at the London Marquee in 1984. I'd just done a solo support to a new American act called Metallica. The autograph hunter, of course, turned out to be Lars. That was the first I'd heard of the band (or thrash). I'd been the vocalist in the Tygers Of Pan Tang and unbeknownst to me Metallica were into us NWOBHM bands in a big way… I've spoken to Lars since and what he doesn't know about the NWOBHM isn't worth knowing. For instance he told me he had bought a Tygers album called *First Kill* in Japan and on it was a track called 'The Final Answer' which is also 'Fireclown' on our *Wild Cat* album but with a different chorus; you really wouldn't know that unless you were a serious NWOBHM train spotter (no offence – sadly I count myself as chief anorak in that queue)."

He went on to say that they would swap tapes and vinyl in the early 1980s of NWOBHM releases with friends who went on to be in Anthrax, Armored Saint and even a young Brian Slagel who would later form Metal Blade Records. Hilariously, Lars also said he'd invite rock kids back to his house where once inside he could force them to listen to the new Tygers, Diamond Head, Holocaust records at lethal volume; apparently James was an early victim of this musical waterboarding!

It's pretty obvious that the whole hard, edgy 'American sounding' bands at the time took their influence from the NWOBHM as the US in 1980 to 1982 was soft rock Toto, Boston and April Wine. No wonder really we were in demand by some American kids who wanted to blow their brains out!"[ci]

John Ricci – guitarist in the cult Canadian speed metal band Exciter – spoke with the author about the first time he saw Metallica live: "That first time was in London at the Marquee Club in 1984, believe it or not. In the spring of 1984 a tour was supposed to take place in Europe called The Hell On Earth Tour, featuring Exciter, Metallica and headliners The Rods (from New York state) but it never happened because the tour was cancelled

at the last minute; the same day we arrived in London. So, our record company at the time, Music For Nations, decided to have us and Metallica stay for two weeks to do press interviews and possibly arrange separate shows for us and Metallica. As a result Metallica played The Marquee to a sold out show, standing room only and in the audience were celebrities Lemmy and Würzel (Motörhead), Kelly Johnson (Girlschool), Jon Sykes (Whitesnake) and others. The audience went totally crazy after every single song and it was so crowded it was difficult to actually stand in the room when Metallica was performing."[cii]

New York shock rockers Twisted Sister joined Venom and Metallica on tour as part of the Seven Dates Of Hell jaunt, which only consisted of sixteen shows despite the seemingly sporadic spread of dates. This tour raised Metallica's profile considerably in Europe especially after they played to 7,000 fans at Aardschok Festival in Zwolle, Netherlands. This was exactly the kind of exposure Metallica needed to make any kind of dent in the European metal scene.

Ride The Lightning opens with the harmonic guitars of 'Fight With Fire'. The song quickly bursts into a whirlwind of electric riffs, bass and drums. The song showed that Metallica had progressed as musicians since they began releasing demo tapes in the early part of the band's history. It's a tremendously powerful song with a profound lyrical subject matter, that of the end of the world, the Armageddon. It has become one of the most recognised songs in Metallica's powerful arsenal. The title track kicks off some thumping drums and bass and a distinctive guitar chord structure. The dual riffs of Hammett and Hetfield recall classic late 1970s Judas Priest and the song really comes into its own about two minutes in, before a melodic middle section and mid-paced tempo is played and there's a catchy guitar solo in there too. Lyrically, the song is about the American criminal justice system; specifically about a prisoner waiting death by electrocution. For the literary minded metal fans out there, 'For Whom The Bell Tolls' is evidently inspired by the novel of the same name by the revered American author Ernest Hemmingway. Lyrically, the song is about modern warfare and the dishonour of it. The introduction is said to be that of Cliff Burton's bass guitar. He played a wah-wah pedal and distorted it, giving it an electric guitar sound. The introduction was believed to have been composed by Burton back in 1979 in his band Agents Of Misfortune during a 'Battle Of The Bands' contest. It really is a tremendous song and one of Metallica's most prized compositions. It has a strong melody and Hetfield's vocals are more apparent and clear, making it easier to understand the lyrics. Suffice to say 'For Whom The Bell Tolls' is a Metallica fan favourite.

Next up is 'Fade To Black' about a man thinking of attempting suicide and then actually committing it. It was a controversial song that many believed was pro-suicide. "When you're up there on stage, anything you say can be taken literally, and you have to be conscious of that," commented Hetfield about the song's premise. "There's a real sick [feeling] of power when you're on stage: you can start a riot or put everyone to sleep if you wanted."[ciii] 'Fade To Black' could be said to be a power ballad; it opens with acoustic guitars before the rest of the band come in and so it gets heavier and more progressive. It proved that the band were far from an average thrash metal outfit; they were more than a one dimensional band. 'Trapped Under Ice' is a fairly obscure song and one that up until the *World Magnetic* Tour in the late noughties had only been played live a handful of times. It opens with a riff before the drums and bass kick in. It's a fast song with some excellent guitars. On the lyrics front, the song is about a man trapped in a cryogenics chamber. The genesis of 'Trapped Under Ice' is an interesting one: it actually dates back to Hammett's former band Exodus and more specifically, a demo called 'Impaler' (Exodus finally released their version of 'Impaler' on 2004s *Tempo Of The Damned*).

'Escape' is about a prisoner on the run for the law and was originally called 'The Hammer'. It's not one of Metallica's most well-known efforts but it certainly has its merits although it does need a more flavoured guitar solo than the one it has. 'Creeping Death' is a sturdy track with some awesome guitar work and though Ulrich's drums are hardly complex they do work competently with the guitars and bass. Lyrically, the track is about the Plague Of The Death Of The First Born from the Biblical passage Exodus 12:29; more specifically about the ten plagues of Egypt.

Finally, the album closes with the epic instrumental 'The Call Of Ktulu' which was their second instrumental after '(Anesthesia) Pulling Teeth' from *Kill 'Em All* ('The Call Of Ktulu' was the last Metallica song to have a co-writing credit by Mustaine. Even though the original name of the song was actually 'When Hell Freezes Over', the finalised version derived its name from the H.P. Lovecraft supernatural novella, *The Call Of Cthulhu*, which was introduced to the rest of the band by Cliff Burton.

The change in spelling to 'Ktulu' was due to the tongue-in-cheek notion that the beast known as Cthulhu would stay away from the band because the name was spelt differently (the original idea being if you spoke the word out loud the beast would come after you; misspelling its name saved your skin!). It's a powerful track with layers of guitars and bass and distortion. A mighty way to finish the opus.

It can be said, emphatically, that *Ride The Lightning* is a bona fide metal masterpiece that hits all the right spots. On this album, Metallica began to develop their own style. Although it is the sound of a young, angry and ambitious band they also sound more seasoned than perhaps anyone would expect of a group who had only crafted one previous album. *Ride The Lightning* contains some of Metallica's most powerful and sturdy riffs and as such is not only rightly regarded as one of their best albums but also as a genre defining release. Hands down: it's a metal masterpiece. How could they follow up this release? Time would tell…

Ride The Lightning was released in August, 1984. It peaked at Number 100 in the *Billboard 200* album charts and Number 87 in the UK Top 100 album chart (in France, the album was wrongly printed with a green rather than blue cover. The 400 green covers released by Bernett Records have become collector's items, highly sought after by fans). It may have made only a minor dent in the charts, but for Metallica it was the beginning of their eventual global chart domination. Despite Dave Mustaine's departure from the band he did receive songwriting credits on 'Ride The Lightning' and 'The Call Of Ktulu'. The album gave birth to the following singles: 'Fade To Black', 'Creeping Death' and 'For Whom The Bell Tolls'.

Critical opinion was more positive than for the band's debut and reviews were also more widespread. However, some Metallica zealots had attacked the band for including a ballad ('Fade To Black') and accused them of selling out. Metal Blade Founder and CEO, Brian Slagel says, "I honestly was not a huge fan of *Kill 'Em All* as I thought James's voice was not quite up to par yet. The music was great of course. *Ride The Lightning* was amazing though and that album really, I thought, launched them big time! It is still my fave Metallica album today."[civ]

Metal Forces' Bernard Doe reflects: "*Ride The Lightning* is over 27 years old [at the time of writing] and songs like 'Creeping Death', 'For Whom The Bell Tolls' and 'Fade To Black' still rank among Metallica's finest work. Actually, I remember the inclusion of the latter prompted the first crys of 'sell-out' and 'wimps' from the underground hordes. So, even early on in 1984 Metallica were upsetting the so-called 'true' metal fans. But the truth was

that they were already publically distancing themselves from the 'thrash' tag and had learnt that you didn't have to depend on speed to remain aggressive and heavy."[cv]

On future reissues, critics and reviewers would rave over the eight track opus. Criticism aimed at the album – such as the sound quality – was almost irrelevant as the band had obviously crafted a strong selection of songs and were more technically adept than they were at the time of the recording of *Kill 'Em All*.

"I think generally most people have received it favourably and certainly a lot better than I think anyone in the band thought it would," Lars Ulrich said at the time.[cvi]

Has the album stood the test of time? Here's what the rock and metal scribes said in the noughties: *Sputnikmusic* declared: "Metallica's sophomore release, *Ride The Lightning*, is a classic thrash album, a classic metal album, and just a regular old classic album in general… The guitar on the album is superb, with some of these riffs being some of Kirk's most memorable. The bass, particularly in 'For Whom The Bell Tolls', is remarkable, and just another reason why Cliff is worshipped by a large portion of Metallica fans. You need to buy this album if you have not yet heard it."

Steve Huey of *MSN Music* stated: "Incredibly ambitious for a one-year-later sophomore effort, *Ride The Lightning* finds Metallica aggressively expanding their compositional technique and range of expression. Every track tries something new, and every musical experiment succeeds mightily. The lyrics push into new territory as well – more personal, more socially conscious, less metal posturing."

The Metal Observer enthused: "Everything fits, sound, songs and atmosphere. And all of this can mean one thing, just like hundreds of other metal journalists have done before: give this album the full rating. Let's just hope that Metallica sometimes might be able to release another hammer like this one, even though I have my doubts…"

However, *Punk News* had some criticisms: "*Ride* really only has two weaknesses: The Judas Priest tribute of 'Escape' sounds dated (even if it is enjoyable), and ending the record with the instrumental 'The Call Of Ktulu' seems to somehow slow the album's momentum even though it's the last song."

Author Martin Popoff says, "Huge effect on me, this album had. I'll never forget dropping the needle on 'Fight Fire With Fire', along with the fact that the same day I brought the import of this record home, I had brought home Savatage (*Sirens*) and

Savage (*Loose 'N Lethal*) forever a weird blue-and-white trio imprinted on my brain. The latter two had their charms, well, more than that, they are a couple of the greatest heavy metal albums of all time. But *Ride The Lightning*… there was a recognition that it was an instant masterpiece, that the rules had changed, or there was a new frontier to be explored for those who were brave enough. Super-fast, progressive, lots of changes, changes in speed, and that was just the first two tracks, which I guess are probably the most masterpiece-like on the album, from a purely showing-off point of view. But yeah, it barely sounded like the same band as the one that made the drinking songs of *Kill 'Em All*, which, yeah, was sort of just like a more-groovy-and-tuneful-than-average German thrash album. This was a pageant of searing Mensa-like metal beyond what anybody had done. Beyond the first two tracks, it then fell to superlative songwriting, and the whole album was enveloped in a remarkable production job, remarkable in that it is both full-spectrum, no faults, and also in that Zeppelin-like manner, obscure and eccentric at the same time, not that Zeppelin ever had that first 'no fault' bit to their otherwise goodly name. But yeah, with *Ride The Lightning*, any idiot metalhead could tell that these guys were far and above the best of the new breed, although most studious metalheads were also likely of the opinion that Metallica really were never going to be huge stars doing this kind of music, because it was just too challenging as well as sounding like two large millstones grinding together. Still, the album is full of catchiness, so who knows? But yeah, the point here was that we were witnessing truckloads of talent from a band who one would think was too young to be this good. This happened exactly twice before, with Mercyful Fate circa *Melissa* and with Judas Priest circa *Sad Wings Of Destiny*. That was my belief anyway, at 21, an instant connection with those records …"[cvii]

The general consensus amongst metal fans is that *Ride The Lightning* is an absolute classic; one of the greatest heavy metal albums in history. Its legacy is most definitely assured. In November, 1987, it was certified Gold while in 2003 it was certified Platinum a staggering five times. *Ride The Lightning* was listed positioned at Number 3 in *Metal-Rules* 'Top 100 Metal Albums Of All Time'. Also, *IGN Music* ranked it at Number 5 in their poll of 'Top 25 Metal Albums'. Even the British music mag *NME* rated it in their poll of 'The 20 Best 80s Metal Albums Ever'. In *Kerrang!*'s '100 Greatest Heavy Metal Albums Of All Time' (published in 1989) *Ride The Lightning* was situated at Number 7 although bizarrely Def Leppard's *Pyromania* was a position ahead! Oddly, in 1998 *Kerrang!* published '100 Albums You Must Hear Before You Die' and had three Metallica albums included, except *Ride The Lightning*.

Looking back, James Hetfield enthused years later: "Overall, I'd have to say *Ride The Lightening* is my favourite. *Kill 'Em All*, our first album, was already written when we went into the studio but *Ride...* was the first next step, when we started to discover the studio and what we could do in it. That was kinda the fun bit, and it still is."[cviii]

Metallica were offered a deal by the UK label Bronze Records but after a few weeks of careful consideration they declined. The biggest and most important event of 1984 was the band's meeting with Michael Alago, Elektra Records A&R representative and Cliff Burnstein, co-founder of Q-Prime Management. These were two of the most influential players in the music industry; both of them attended a Metallica gig in September and were so impressed with the performance that they signed the band to their respective labels. However, the band themselves were not that impressed with their performance. "It was really funny, because as soon as we got off stage we all agreed it was probably one of the worst gigs we'd ever done!"[cix]

Metallica were pleased with Burnstein who was known for his work with AC/DC, Def Leppard and Dokken and would in time help turn Metallica into a global force. Over the coming years and many albums and tours, it would prove to be a powerful partnership. Also, Elektra Records would give a lot of time, effort and money into promoting their new band; it wasn't one of those huge record companies where bands get lost in an extensive catalogue of artists, so every artist was treated with the same degree of energy and enthusiasm and given ample time.

Also, the strength of the musicianship on *Ride The Lightning* particularly impressed them. Metallica's star was rising. Indeed this was a major coup for the band and in Britain, Music For Nations were so enthusiastic about Metallica's growing success that they released a limited edition version of the 'Creeping Death' single with Diamond Head's 'Am I Evil?' and Blitzkrieg's 'Blitzkrieg' as B-sides (Both 'Am I Evil?' and 'Blitzkrieg' were included on the 1989 Elektra reissue of *Kill 'Em All*). As an import in the United States, 'Creeping Death' sold a whopping 40,000 copies!

Blitzkrieg's Brian Ross reflected his second encounter with Metallica to the author: "My next contact with Metallica was when Lars called Neat Records to get my home telephone number so that he could call me. He did call me, and after an oratory of how much a fan he was of mine and Blitzkrieg, he asked if I would give Metallica permission to do a cover of the song 'Blitzkrieg'. I gave my permission and the rest as they say is history. Since that time I have always made sure that my record company has sent them a copy of each album that I have recorded. I met them briefly at Donington Festival. That was the year [1991] that AC/DC headlined and Queensrÿche and Mötley Crüe were also on the bill. As yet, I have never got up on stage with them to play 'Blitzkrieg' but I would love to do it. Who knows? One day I may get the chance!"[cx]

Lars Ulrich had become Metallica's (un)official spokesman, often doing the majority of interviews and speaking in public on the band's behalf. It took some time before James Hetfield felt as comfortable talking to the press. "There was a point around *Ride The Lightning* where I felt that I was being misquoted, I didn't understand the press game," he admitted. "My remedy was just not to do it. It was the worst thing because then they make up shit. It's always better to sound like your own idiot than someone else's."[cxi]

Bernard Doe who co-founded and edited the UK magazine *Metal Forces* told the author about his relationship with Ulrich: "The first time I met and interviewed Lars Ulrich was the day after he arrived in the UK ahead off the band's first European tour with Venom in 1984, and over the next ten years I interviewed him several times for *Metal Forces*. I remember after each interview in those early days Lars would nearly always call me at home a couple of days later and ask me to change or leave some comments out that he had made about an individual or another band. Lars was very conscious of trying to remain diplomatic and not upset anyone back then. I've always got on well with Lars and I think that we had a mutual respect for one another. He spent a lot of time in Europe, and in particular London, when Metallica were not touring. There were many drunken nights out on the town, and I have the photos to prove it!"[cxii]

Doe continued: "Lars also had a habit of turning up in Shades record store in London just as they were about to close so he could blag some free records! He was always asking about my New Wave Of British Heavy Metal record collection. I remember he was after a copy of the Trespass 'One Of These Days' 7" single. It wasn't a particular rare record, but I had a copy with a picture sleeve which he didn't have. Lars actually agreed to trade an official Metallica RIAA Gold Album Award for my copy of that Trespass single![cxiii]

On November 16, the band kicked off the Bang Your Head That Doesn't Bang Tour with support from the cult British metal band Tank (Bang That Head That Doesn't Bang was printed on the top of the back of the original pressing of Metallica's debut album but was dropped on the 1988 reissue and later versions). This was Metallica's first major headlining tour of Europe where they played to around 1,300 fans each night; they played at the Lyceum Theatre in London on December 20 and to spruce up the bill Torme were added to that date – they did not open the evening, instead Tank came onstage first followed by Torme before Metallica played their headlining slot. Much of Metallica's set was dominated by the interplay between Hetfield and Ulrich with Hammett playing the lead breaks. Ulrich has perhaps never been the most technical drummer, not on a par with such acknowledged virtuosos as say, Neil Peart of Rush or perhaps Nicko McBrain from Iron Maiden. "It was always a kind of

P.L.P. Present
METALLICA
Plus Support
LYCEUM BALLROOM
THURS. 20th DEC. 7.30
Tickets £3.50
Over Eighteens only Admitted on this ticket
№ 1700

contest – who could down-pick the fastest – and mostly it was a battle between me and Lars, actually," said Hetfield. "It's a hard thing to do well, because your timing has got to be dead on... If you're playing eighth or sixteenth notes then you've got to get cooking. A lot of practice is called for to build up your strength."[cxiv]

Another one of Metallica's primary metal influences was the metal legends Judas Priest. Certainly one of the greatest and most inspirational metal bands of all time, Judas Priest formed in the English Midlands in 1969 but after several line-up changes and a complicated beginning, the iconic line-up of singer Rob Halford, guitarists K.K. Downing and Glenn Tipton and bassist Ian Hill with a revolving line-up of drummers was cemented by the mid-1970s. They pioneered the dual guitar attack and the whole landscape of heavy metal was changed with albums like *Sin After Sin* in 1977, *Stained Class* in 1978 and *Killing Machine* (aka *Hell Bent For Leather*) in 1979. Though they compromised their heavier, darker metal sound in the 1980s, Judas Priest have never been shy about trying and adapting to new sounds within the metal landscape and certainly their diversity inspired Ulrich.

Jeff Waters of the Canadian thrash band Annihilator told the author in 2006 that Judas Priest had a massive impact on the North American metal scene: "What grabbed me about Priest is that they can do anything! I mean, you look at some bands – and some of my favourites bands [are] Slayer, Metallica, Enemy and Maiden. Maiden and Metallica, they can change styles... But Priest is able to do fifty different styles in one band and that's what really turned me on to heavy metal music... that K.K. [Downing] and [Glenn] Tipton could do classical, influenced stuff and then they could do the... blues-influenced things."[cxv]

One particular album by Judas Priest that had an enormous impact on the American thrash metal bands of the early 1980s such as Metallica and Anthrax was *British Steel*. Anthrax guitarist and Judas Priest fan Scott Ian told *Metal Hammer* and subsequently the author of this book: "*British Steel* was a huge influence on and precursor to what the Big Four of American thrash would become. It's one of those perfect records at the perfect time. Picking up from where they left off on *Hell Bent* [*For Leather* aka *Killing Machine*,] Priest kicked metal in the ass with songs like 'Rapid Fire' and 'Steeler' and set the bar (that they had already set) even higher. The overall energy on this record is unlike any other Priest record, the tracks literally jumping off the record into my ears all driven by Tipton and Downing's iconic riffs and Halford's insane vocals. In 1980 it was state of the art and it absolutely holds up today."[cxvi]

Metallica ended the Bang That Head That Doesn't Bang Tour on December 20 after 25 dates. The band would soon be a force to be reckoned with on a global scale...

METALLICA

W.A.S.P

ARMORED SAINT

City Coliseum

THURSDAY FEB. 21, 1985

A ROADSTAR Production
Special Assistance by WATCHTOWER

Tickets: WATERLOO RECORDS—INNER SANCTUM RECORDS—DISCOUNT RECORDS—BOTH PAT MCGEES—HENRYS MEMRYS AND AT THE DOOR DAY OF SHOW—DOORS OPEN: 7:30 PM

Master of Puppets
1985-1986

"I'm glad bands like Metallica and Slayer have been signed to major labels, because that has opened a lot of doors for the whole new wave of metal that's around right now. I don't know if thrash will ever reach a point where you'll here [sic] it being played on the radio as often as genesis or anything like that, but at the moment it seems to be picking up popularity and that's a good thing, I think."

James Newsted[cxvii]

Metallica kicked off the *Ride The Lightning* Tour on January 9, 1985, with co-headliners W.A.S.P. in the United States and support came from Armored Saint and Tank on selected dates (W.A.S.P. dropped out of the tour to support KISS on a major arena tour of the States). Jeff Waters of Annihilator, a Metallica fan, remembered: "A Metallica tour I remember seeing, which was fantastic, [was] with Armored Saint and W.A.S.P."[cxviii]

1984 was a year of numerous behind-the-scenes legal issues in the US for the band and so they chose to concentrate virtually all of their live activity in Europe.[cxix] During the 57 date tour, Metallica regularly played the following set-list: 'Fight Fire With Fire', 'Ride The Lightning', 'Phantom Lord', 'The Four Horsemen', '(Anesthesia) Pulling Teeth', 'For Whom The Bell Tolls', 'No Remorse', 'Fade To Black', 'Seek & Destroy', 'Whiplash', 'Creeping Death', 'Am I Evil?' and 'Motorbreath'.

The tour included a performance in front of 70,000 metal maniacs at the Monsters Of Rock Festival at Castle Donington in England on August 17 where they came second from bottom of the bill after the Midlands pomp rock band Magnum. Other notable acts on the bill included Ratt, Marillion and headliners Bon Jovi. "British audiences though are strange," said Ulrich. "But once you've convinced yourselves that just because you're

being bombarded with two litre bottles of full piss, mud and ham sandwiches doesn't meant that they don't like you…"[cxx]

Metallica also performed in front of 60,000 fans at California's Day At The Green Festival on August 31 with the Scorpions, Ratt, Y&T and Rising Force also on the bill. They felt more comfortable playing back in the States where people were more familiar with their music.

Despite the aforementioned heavy touring commitments, Metallica had laid down some further demos for what was to be their third album on July 15, 1985. They would begin recording tracks at Copenhagen's Sweet Silence Studios – where they had crafted *Ride The Lightning* – on September 1. They were unhappy with the studios in LA where bands were given tight recording schedules so they chose to go back to the country of Ulrich's youth, Denmark. However, the band had gone into the studio too early with the current state of songwriting. A more organised schedule and better preparation would have been preferable. They would wind up those recording sessions on December 27 with the final date of the *Ride The Lightning* Tour arriving on December 31, 1985.

Cliff Burton: "It [recording] took too long. We didn't manage our time all that well, but the songs were all real good and what we came out with was very good. Like I said, we could've managed our time a bit better, but all in all it was, I think, quite a success."[cxxi]

Burton had started to spend some time playing guitar and he'd play licks and riffs from well-known songs and get the rest of the band to figure out what he was playing. Burton was a big fan of so many different types of bands: Black Sabbath, Misfits, Creedence Clearwater Revival, Eagles, The Velvet Underground, the Sex Pistols and Thin Lizzy. He introduced the 1974 Thin Lizzy album *Night Life* to Kirk Hammett when the guitarist was more of a fan of latterday Lizzy like *Bad Reputation*, *Jailbreak* and *Renegade* but he was impressed with Burton's knowledge of music history. Burton turned Hetfield and Hammett on to a lot of other bands too. He knew how to bring harmonies into a song and brought that aspect to *Master Of Puppets*. He'd often write down harmonies on bits of paper and planned the songs in his head. Classical music was also a big influence on him which can be heard on forthcoming third album, *Master Of Puppets*.

"I remember him [Burton] playing me these volume-swell things that he had come up with and that we later used as the intro to 'Damage, Inc.' from *Master Of Puppets*," Hammett explained. "He told me it was based on some Bach piece, and that it had a death theme to it, some funeral march thing."[cxxii]

James Hetfield commented years later on the band's method of recording: "We can be at separate ends of the studio – I will say one thing, and Lars will be on the other end, saying the exact opposite. It's not on purpose. I wish it was. Then we could coordinate it. But that's how Metallica have always worked. There's a tug of war, a constant battle, and it ends up in the middle somewhere, where each of us can live with it."[cxxiii]

Again, they'd hooked up with producer Flemming Rasmussen with the legendary Michael Wagener mixing. The band had planned to have Rasmussen mix the album but they ran over schedule and so with Rasmussen moving on to other projects, and after playing a low-key warm-up gig in preparation for the forthcoming tour with Y&T and Armored Saint, they recruited the excellent Wagener for mixing.

"Cliff Bernstein from Q-Prime management contacted me and asked if I was interested. I was," says Wagener. "If I remember it right, about two weeks, normal time for an album mix... They knew exactly what they wanted to hear. The whole session went pretty easy, no major problems… At the time this was the heaviest album I had done. We had a lot of fun during the process. I am very happy that it went so well for them."[cxxiv]

Moving in to the New Year, Hetfield had joined a party band called Spastic Children with Fred Cotton on vocals, James McDaniels on guitar, and a bassist named Jumbo. They played some shows in the San Francisco area in early 1986.

Even though Hetfield had another outlet for his talents, Metallica had spent longer working on *Master Of Puppets* than they had on their first two albums which resulted in a longer wait between releases. Fans were eager for new material. Lars Ulrich explained after the album's release: "I mean a lot of bands go into the studio, find the right guitar or drum sound and then bash it out, particularly with the first album. But if you listen to *Master Of Puppets* you can hear a lot of different moods and feels, so sometimes we would work for maybe one or two days on just getting the right guitar sound for a specific part of a song."[cxxv]

Master Of Puppets opens with the five-minute-long 'Battery' written by Hetfield and Ulrich. The intro is similar to that of 'Fight Fire With Fire' in that there are harmonic acoustic guitars with an almost Spanish feel, before the thrash metal electric riffs burst into action. The tempo speeds up considerably and the drums, though not technically amazing or especially innovative, accompany the riffs with enough speed and angst to maintain the song's strength. The central guitar solo is a killer and adds more fuel to the fire. 'Battery' remains one of Metallica's most accomplished thrash metal creations. Lyrically, the subject matter matches the speed and frustration in the song as it's about anger management. 'Master Of Puppets' – purported to be bassist Cliff Burton's favourite song on the album – is about drugs and how they take hold of the consumer. It's a tremendous piece of work and has gone down in metal history as one of the greatest riffs and metal songs ever. About three and a half minutes into the track, the tempo slows down and there is some harmonic but complex instrumentation which makes it similar in a sense to

'Ride The Lightning'. However, the thrash metal attack starts up again and it finishes with a huge climax. 'The Thing That Should Not Be' may be one of the album's least well-known tracks but it remains a stomping metallic monster with a fine riff and some interesting tempo changes. The next track is 'Welcome Home (Sanitarium)' which is another angry, angst-ridden song. It begins with a slow tempo and vocals before the thrash metal attack commences and the bass and drums thrust into action. It was apparently written by Hetfield as a tribute to the film *One Flew Over The Cuckoo's Nest*; the song being about a person trapped in a mental health institution. About four minutes into the song and the riff evokes Rush's 'Tom Sawyer' and that band's influence on the group is respectfully acknowledged with a thank you in the album's sleeve notes (Interestingly, some knowledgeable rock fans have noted how Rush's 'Tom Sawyer' similarly evokes Journey's 'Nickel And Dime' (instrumental) from their third album *Next*, which was released in 1977). It's a powerful song that ends with layers of guitars.

Keeping the pace going, 'Disposable Heroes' is a very fast track, furiously filled with Motörhead-style riffs like machine gun ammunition. It's a musically complex song at a little over eight minutes long, with more layers of guitars. The song opens with some fantastic instrumentation. As with 'No Remorse' from *Kill 'Em All* and 'For Whom The Bell Tolls' from *Ride The Lightning*, the subject matter in 'Disposable Heroes' concerns war and the experiences and thoughts and emotions of a soldier at war (The recording of 'Disposable Heroes' goes back to 1985 when it was first demoed. One of the riffs from the slightly longer demo version was later used on 'Damage, Inc.'). 'Leper Messiah' is an almost six-minute-long metal musical rant that has a stomping riff and Hetfield's vocals are terrifically pronounced on this track. 'Orion' is an eight-minute instrumental which houses some of Burton's distinctive bass playing; he manages to make his bass sound like a lead guitar so much so that the two bass solos actually sound like lead guitar. However, there are a couple of guitar solos in the song by Hammett and Hetfield, separately. There's a heavy progressive element to 'Orion' which makes it one of Metallica's most indelible tracks ('Orion' was constructed from bits of other songs the band had abandoned, for example the middle section). However, 'Orion' really belongs to bassist Cliff Burton who excels throughout the track. The album ends with 'Damage, Inc.' which is a monster of a song, totally destructive with rapid firing riffs and speedy drums. It's the perfect way to finish the album as it displays Metallica in all their metal glory.

On the whole, *Master Of Puppets* is a committed masterpiece from start to finish; a fully-committed thrash metal onslaught. It's like an assault on the senses; it's non-stop. It is easy to overpraise this album but many metal fans have concluded that it is practically flawless in its execution and displays some of the band's most brilliant riffs. It is also more versatile than the band's previous two albums with lots of unique chord innovations and unusual basslines. They also show a strong sense of musicality in that they'd progressed steadily as musicians in what was a relatively short period of time. James Hetfield's voice had also certainly developed hugely since the first album with more vocal harmonies than growls.

Master Of Puppets is an angry album, both musically and lyrically. "I mean, let's face it, the world is not a pretty place," Hammett said in 1986. "The world is pretty sick. There's a lot of ugly things out there and no matter how much you try and escape you always have to wake up and face the fact that the world is fucked-up and ugly."[cxxvi]

James Hetfield: "Some of the stuff... well *Master Of Puppets* deals pretty much with drugs. How things get switched around, instead of you controlling what you're taking and doing it's drugs controlling you. Like, I went to a party here in S.F. [San Francisco], there were all these freaks shooting up and geezin' [drinking] and this other girl was real sick."[cxxvii]

They began experimenting with words and even making up their own words. The band were young, angry and had a lot to say and music was the best way of venting their anger. It was certainly preferable to violence and being street thugs hanging around corner blocks. Hetfield said years later: "Well, I think

I understand feelings more now but I don't think I've mellowed or anything. Some of the earlier stuff was just, 'I got shit in me and it's coming out – look out!'"[cxxviii]

What begin with *Kill 'Em All* was built upon with *Ride The Lightning* but with *Master Of Puppets* it's like the band had jumped ten steps ahead. Those first two albums were/are not exactly weak though they do have their minor flaws. However *Master Of Puppets* in many fans' eyes remains their finest achievement to date. However, in 1988, Lars Ulrich told journalist Richard Gehr: "*Puppets* was very well recorded and had a very huge sort of sound, but didn't really fuckin' come out of the speakers and hit you in the face."[cxxix]

When asked about Burton's influence on the band's first three albums, Joel McIver, author of the critically revered best-selling Cliff Burton biography *To Live Is To Die,* says, "Not on the sound as such, because his bass wasn't mixed that high. He definitely added a touch of virtuosity, though, thanks to songs like 'Orion' and the bass solos on 'The Call Of Ktulu' and 'For Whom The Bell Tolls.'"[cxxx]

Master Of Puppets was released in March, 1986. It peaked at Number 29 in the American *Billboard* 200 album charts but like most classic albums sales kept steady over the years. The album sold 300,000 copies in its first four weeks of release and it spent a lengthy 72 weeks in the charts in the United States. It would become one of the band's most enduring albums (*Master Of Puppets* was certified Gold in November, 1986 and it was certified Platinum six times in 2003). It peaked at Number 41 in the UK. The band were slowly climbing the charts with each subsequent release. Metallica unleashed 'Master Of Puppets', 'Battery' and 'Welcome Home (Sanitarium)' as singles. Yet despite their success they had not yet made a music video nor would any radio station play their music. To many people, Metallica was a scary creation. The band liked being outsiders, lone wolves of the music world. Like many of their idols, they craved a cult underground status rather than worldwide mainstream adulation. They were a metal band through and through. Would that kind of appeal and image last?

Critical opinion was high. Suffice to say *Master Of Puppets* remains Metallica's most accomplished work; at least that is the general consensus of Metallica fans and metal followers in general. However, Metallica were not concerned with the critics or even their own fanbase. "I don't know if people will believe this or not," said Lars Ulrich in an interview with *Metal Forces*' Bernard Doe in 1986, "but we write and play for ourselves, we're really not consciously trying to please anyone else, we just go about pleasing ourselves and it just seems that we have a tendency to please other people as well."[cxxxi]

"*Master Of Puppets* is an absolute classic album which really put Metallica in a league of their own in terms of the whole thrash movement that was booming at the time," *Metal Forces*' Bernard Doe told the author. "The material was generally more complex and more varied, but the songs retained that 'crunching' heaviness that had become Metallica's trademark. Also, the album saw James Hetfield develop into a more confident vocalist."[cxxxii]

On subsequent reissues, the album still garners high praise and its position in the pantheon of metal albums is more than assured. The album's legacy will outlive the band. The success and reverence bestowed upon the album has meant the band has achieved immortality; as long as metal lasts, this album will be remembered.

Here's what the rock and metal scribes said in the noughties: *Metal Archives* said: "Very few albums can stand the test of time like this album does. People have a very biased opinion on Metallica but let's forget all that. This was before the *St. Anger* abomination and well before they sued Napster or headlined Lollapalooza and toured with Limp Bizkit and Linkin Park. This was Metallica, the young band who were hungry and produced a truly remarkable, timeless album for generations to come."

Metal Storm enthused: "From the intro of 'Battery' to the last guitar riff of 'Damage, Inc.', the CD is just perfect, incredible and all the adjectives you want. In this album Metallica composed the song of songs: 'Master Of Puppets', astonishing. Eight minutes 38 seconds of pure metal. The virtuosity composing of Metallica appears clearly in that song. In *Master Of Puppets* (maybe influenced by Black Sabbath) some songs are really dark and paranoid like 'The Thing That Should Not Be'."

Steve Huey of *All Music* stated: "By bookending the album with two slices of thrash mayhem ('Battery' and 'Damage, Inc.') the band reigns triumphant through sheer force – of sound, of will, of malice. The arrangements are thick and muscular, and the material varies enough in texture and tempo to hold interest through all its twists and turns. Some critics have called *Master Of Puppets* the best heavy metal album ever recorded; if it isn't, it certainly comes close."

BBC.co.uk pointed out some of the album's themes: "It's hard, fast rock with substance that doesn't require the listener to wear eye-liner or big fire-hazard hair to enjoy. It also features more serious themes (albeit expressed in a particularly aggressive and direct way) and more complex arrangements than similar acts of the same era."

Martin Popoff gave the author of this book his take on the band's third mighty opus: "I did a book called *The Top 500 Heavy Metal Albums Of All Time*, and the ranking was purely something that fell out of a poll. This album took Number 1. Obviously, amazing album, but I remember feeling at the time, and still feeling, being I guess old school and maybe even a little jaded by 1986, that *Master Of Puppets*, great album that it is, was really just a refinement or a tuning up over *Ride The Lightning*. As one is wont to do as a kid, Metallica made it easy to order one's universe, instrumental against instrumental, the fast, punky, irreverent ones, the catchy mid-paced ones, the epic with vocals. There was almost a complete album to album match-up of the songs on this 'new and improved' Metallica album, over the last one. I dunno, there was a vague more of the same, but yeah, two *Ride The Lightning*'s was better than almost anything else, [better] than one and something else, so no complaints! So I think the second album is way more of a groundbreaker, but *Master Of Puppets* is killer – great in its own way, highly utilitarian. Perhaps the production is a shade better, more bite, maybe even a little more obstinate and underground, but I love both knob jobs. Another impression I do take away is that this record's tour was the first time I saw Metallica live, with Metal Church backing up, and it was one of the most ferocious, face-flung live performances I can recall (Jason was on bass). And much to one's amazement, flying the flag for metal all these years, here is a band that was actually headlining hockey barns, although not nearly full ones, with the big stage show, with pretty darn extreme music. It was a musing like an early version of the marvel at seeing Pantera, Slayer and Slipknot so high in the charts, or selling lots of records."[cxxxiii]

It was Metallica's first major label release so it got more of a promotional plug than *Kill 'Em All* and *Ride The Lightning*. It was their first album to be awarded Gold status having sold over half a million copies. In the States it was awarded Platinum status six times and five times Platinum in Canada.

The fact that *Master Of Puppets* is so highly revered and spoken about in metal circles means it has quite a legacy. It has given the band much mainstream attention over the years. *TIME* magazine in the States listed it in 'The All-TIME 100 Albums' poll in 2006 while *Q* magazine and the acclaimed reference book *1001 Albums You Must Hear Before You Die* also gave it hefty coverage. *IGN* went so far as to place it at Number 1 in their list of 'Top 25 Metal Albums' in 2007 and *Rolling Stone* also placed it (at Number 157) in their poll, 'The 500 Greatest Albums Of All Time'. Other polls the album has featured in include *Guitar World*'s 'The Greatest Guitar Solos' where they positioned the title track at Number 51 while said magazine also positioned the album at Number 4 in a poll of great guitar albums. *Total Guitar* magazine has also rated the album highly in polls dedicated to great riffs. In 2006, *Kerrang!* magazine even went so far as to dedicate a special issue of the magazine to *Master Of Puppets* called *A 20th Anniversary Tribute – Kerrang! Presents Remastered: Metallica's Master Of Puppets Revisited*. The editors of the magazine asked various artists to review each track on the album including Machine Head, Trivium, Mendeed, Bullet For My Valentine, Chimaira, Fightstar, Mastodon and Funeral For A Friend. The lists could go on and on but essentially the album's quality has guaranteed it an enduring and lengthy legacy, not just within the confines of metal.

Songs from the album have also been covered by an array of artists including, but not limited to, the following: Machine Head, Dream Theater, Apocalyptica and Pendulum. The appeal of the album is staggering and has not diminished over the years but in fact has grown in stature and influence. The aforementioned

American progressive metal band Dream Theater went so far as to cover the entire album in concert. It is something the band has done with other artists' masterpieces, including complex works such as Deep Purple's *Made In Japan* and Pink Floyd's *Dark Side Of The Moon*.

Matt Harvey of Exhumed, the American death metal band who released their debut album *Gore-Metal* in 1998, spoke about the influence that *Master Of Puppets* had on him in an excellent interview with Justin M Norton for the *Hellhound* website: "I got the twelve tapes for a penny deal in *Hit Parader* and one of the tapes was *Master Of Puppets*. I remember putting it on and I was like: 'Fuck, something just happened!' That night my whole life direction changed. I was like: 'OK, cool. This is what I'm into now.' From there things got heavier and heavier."[cxxxiv]

Lars Ulrich later said: "Looking back, personally, even though most people say that *Master Of Puppets* was the definitive Metallica album, I think I would probably take *Ride The Lightning* as my most favourite album. Not that I'm gonna criticise the other stuff. You know I hate all that shit when people say like 'Well, that band on the first album is not really for us.' Fuck you it was, it's got your band name right here. It cringes me when people talk like that."[cxxxv]

To celebrate the album's twentieth anniversary in 2006, the band played the record in its entirety at several shows during the Escape From The Studio Tour. They even played a complete performance of the instrumental 'Orion' for the first time which was dedicated to Cliff Burton. Needless to say at those shows the audiences went wild!

With the success of the three albums, Metallica's days of being broke were over: "Now I get to buy the comics I've been wanting since I was a little kid," Kirk Hammett said in 1986. "I can pay more attention now to my hobbies. When I was younger, I was always into comics and I never had enough money to buy *Fantastic Four* Number 1, which I just got today, because of the price."[cxxxvi] He continued: "I do buy certain comics as investments, but I'm not into this hobby just to make money. That sucks, that's more like a broker or something. I don't buy it as much for the monetary value, though, as I do for just sentimental reasons and from a collector's point of view."[cxxxvii]

The band commenced the Damage, Inc. Tour on March 27 by supporting Ozzy Osbourne throughout most of the USA dates leading up to the final show in the States on August 3. Ozzy was promoting his *The Ultimate Sin* album at the time. It would be Metallica's last support slot before they became headliners themselves.

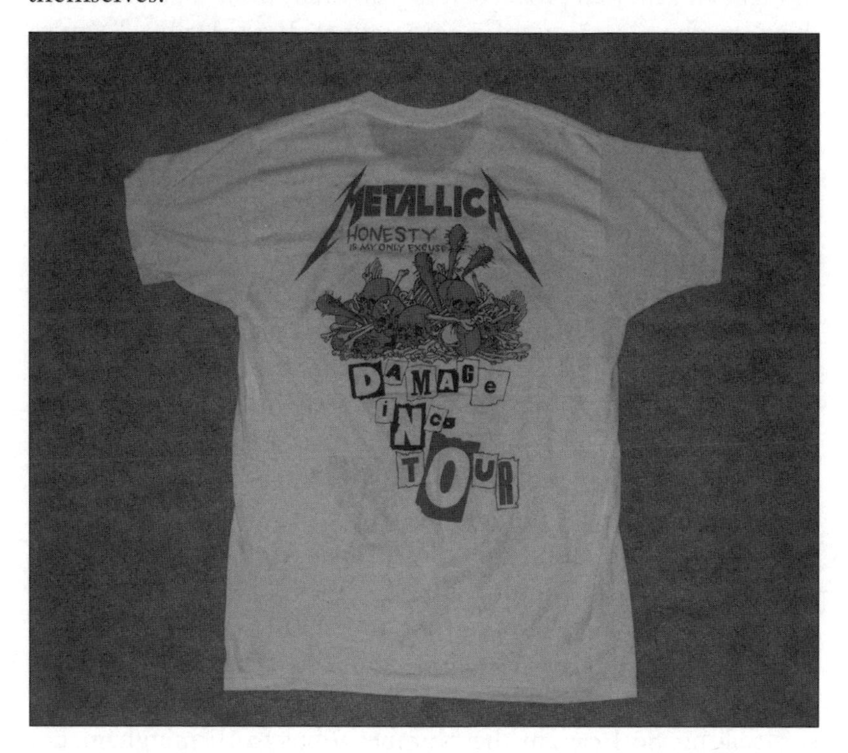

James Hetfield recalled Ozzy's hospitality to *Metal Hammer* in 1999: "We went out and did *Master Of Puppets*. He gave us full reign on the stage and sound-checks every night; we got our backdrop and little crosses up behind us. We would get up and play Black Sabbath songs and hope he would get up and jam with us, but we knew it wasn't going to happen. He thought we were taking the piss when in fact we were honouring him."[cxxxviii]

Speaking to the author, former *Kerrang!* journalist and Metallica chronicler Xavier Russell recalled an 'on the road' story from the Damage, Inc. Tour: "My favourite Metallica article was an 'on the road' feature I did for *Extra Kerrang!* in 1986/7. The band were playing on a double bill with Armored Saint. The Saint possessed a very gifted bassist by the name of Joey Vera, who was later offered the Metallica gig when Cliff tragically died, but remained loyal to the Saint cause. As it was a 'road feature,' we needed a shot on the bus." Russell asked the band what they thought and they all proceeded to pull their knobs out and aimed them in the direction of photographer Ross Halfin. "You've never seen a man or a camera move so fast! He clicked one black and white group shot... Needless to say the picture was used in the finished article."[cxxxix]

The road jaunt would not go without its troubles. Whilst relaxing one day, frontman James Hetfield broke his wrist during a skateboarding accident which prevented him from playing guitar; he continued to sing whilst his guitar tech John Marshall played guitar (John Marshall later became a member of the band, Metal Church). This would not be the first incident on the Damage, Inc. Tour; things would only get worse ... much worse.

The band flew over the Atlantic for the European leg of the tour, beginning on September 10 with support from Anthrax. "We tour because it's fun and because that's what we know and that's what we do best, I think," explained Hetfield.[cxl]

Speaking to the author, Brian Tatler of Diamond Head remembered an anecdote from this tour: "On September 20, Lars called me to say that Metallica (supported by Anthrax) were playing that night at the Birmingham Odeon and would I like to come along. So I caught the Number 9 bus to Birmingham, got my backstage pass and a crew guy took me to see Lars. It was the first time we had met up since 1981, and boy, how times had changed! Lars introduced me to James Hetfield, Kirk Hammett and Cliff Burton, we chatted and Lars suggested I play 'Am I Evil?' onstage with them. Well, why not? Lars said they would be playing it in the encore and suggested that I go and watch the show but come back towards the end of the set. They opened with 'Battery' and I could not get over the energy coming from the band and the enthusiasm of the audience. I had played this

venue myself but this crowd was definitely crazier than a Diamond Head audience. I thought that Metallica were still quite small, but this night changed all that. I didn't know any of the songs and my first thoughts were that it was terrifically fast and complicated (Lars had sent me a cassette of the new album but I hadn't got into it at that point). They were all so much in synch, I remember thinking that if one of them were to leave, how on earth would the remaining members be able to replace him?

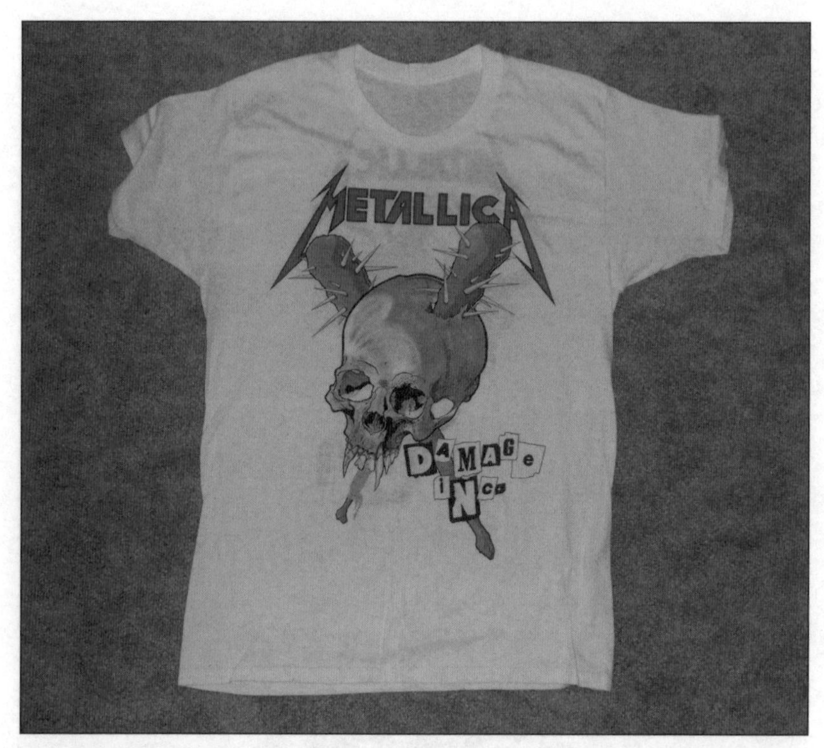

After about an hour I went backstage – still wondering how Lars could play that fast – where the guitar tech strapped James's white Flying V onto me and then I was being introduced as 'The guy who wrote this next song.' The five of us played 'Am I Evil?' up to the fast section, at which point Metallica went into 'Damage Inc.' and I scampered offstage."[cxli]

Tragedy would hit the band on September 27. During the European leg of the Damage, Inc. Tour, members of the band drew cards to see which bunk in the tour bus they would sleep on because they were frustrated with their own bunks, which were presumably uncomfortable. Bassist Cliff Burton chose to sleep in Kirk Hammett's bunk as he won the game with an Ace Of Spades. In Ljungby Municipalityn, near Dörarp in Sweden, the tour bus lost control in the early hours of the morning just before 7a.m. and the vehicle skidded several times causing it to successively flip over. While Ulrich, Hetfield and Hammett escaped with minor cuts and bruises, Cliff Burton was killed.

Burton was thrown outside of the bus, which landed on top of him. Fate had quite literally dealt Burton a shitty card.

Burton's last appearance with Metallica onstage was at the Solnahallen Arena in Stockholm, Sweden on September 26 whilst it was also Hetfield's first show playing guitar since his accident. Burton was cremated on October 7, 1986 and his ashes were spread at Maxwell Ranch (Perhaps the most well-known tribute comes from Megadeth. Dave Mustaine penned 'In My Darkest Hour' which features on *So Far, So Good… So What!* released 1988). Some parties reported ice on the surface but whatever the cause, no charges were brought against the bus driver who was deemed not at fault for the accident.

Could the band continue without Cliff? Would carrying on the Metallica name without Burton be the right thing to do? Should they follow AC/DC after the death of Bon Scott and find a replacement or call it a day like Led Zeppelin after John Bonham's death? It was a decision they could not decide alone…

"My relationship with death is different," Hetfield has said. "I grew up with Christian Science where you don't believe in funerals. In a way it's very unhealthy not to get closure, time to mourn. But the idea behind it is to let the person live on within you. I know that Cliff lives on within us."[cxlii]

Burton's premature and tragic death created an obviously huge void within the realms of the band and it wasn't a case of replacing him – because that would have been impossible given his talent and importance in the early years of Metallica; his bass literally shaped the sound of the band – but about finding a different *type* of bassist. In other words that particular sound on the first three Metallica albums died with him.

Metal Blade's Brian Slagel says, "Cliff was a great guy! A bit quiet, but super cool. He knew his metal also and I think he had a huge influence on how Metallica sounded. And an amazing player and stage presence!"[cxliii]

Photographer Bill Hale tells a story about his relationship with Burton: "I met Cliff way before the band played up here [San Francisco Bay Area]. Even saw Trauma once! Cliff was anything you ever read about him. Cliff was cool, Cliff dug music, Cliff was

Cliff! Right around the release of *Ride* [*The Lightning*] our friendship started to get strained a bit. We both started to get some success. But *MRV* [*Metal Rendezvous* magazine] had not done a proper article on Metallica. Also, I had not shot the band since 1983. At first it was just playful posturing but then it got more aggressive. We would almost come to blows! This went on for awhile but hey, that's life…"[cxliv]

Hale continues: "So Megadeth rolls into town and is opening for King Diamond at The Stone. I'm finishing up my photo session with Megadeth when I see Cliff walk in. 'Oh, great,' I tell myself, and get ready for round 25 with Cliff but he comes up to me and gives me a big bear hug and tells me how great it was to see me! I get some pics with him and Dave hanging out with the King Diamond guys. On the way home I'm thinking what was up with Cliff? A few short weeks later, Cliff was dead! As I recall, Cliff was the first one of us to pass on. The next time I saw Lars and James was at a Megadeth gig a few weeks after Cliff passed. Lars was OK but James was a mess. [I] talked to Dave and he was pissed off. Life as we (The Bay Area) [knew it] would never be the same again…"[cxlv]

With the blessing of Burton's family and some careful thought, Metallica decided that they would continue the band with the understanding that Burton would not want them to dissolve Metallica. "The spirit of this band has always been about fighting on," said Ulrich, "against all the shit we've always run into. Cliff, more than anyone else in the band, would have been the first guy to give us a kick in the ass, and wouldn't want us to sit around."[cxlvi]

Metallica held auditions in California for a new bassist. Over fifty musicians tried out, including Les Claypool of Primus and Troy Gregory of Prong. After Armored Saint's *Raising Fear* recording sessions, the band contacted bassist Joey Vera about replacing the late Cliff Burton but nothing came of it; that would have been an interesting collaboration considering the heaviness of Armored Saint.

Also amongst the auditionees was a dude named James Newsted, Flotsam And Jetsam's bassist. He recalled: "My friend woke me up at six in the morning and said, 'Cliff's gone.' I said,

'No fucking way. Why are you doing this to me this early in the morning?' And he said, 'No, it's real. Go look in the paper.'" Like everyone else, Newsted was mortified to hear of Cliff's death; some time later, when the shock had started to wear off, he began to wonder what this might mean for his own future. "I had this epiphany watching and just thinking and I was like, 'I'm going to be the dude. I'm going to do it. If they're going to go on then I'm the man. I'm going to do it.' And from that minute on I wasn't going to let anybody else get it."[cxlvii]

During the audition period, Newsted went so far as to learn the entire Metallica set-list and so impressed was the band with the bassist that they invited him to Tommy's Joint in San Francisco after the auditions. "I was one of the biggest fans of the band before I went in," Newsted told *Rolling Stone*.[cxlviii]

Metallica played their first live performance with new bassist James Newsted at the County Club in Reseda, California. Such was the humour and mischief between the members that they tricked Newsted into eating some wasabi (Japanese horseradish) as a kind of initiation test.

James Newsted: "Well, naturally somebody had to be able to be strong enough to take on what was about to happen. Not just somebody that could play but somebody that also was able to take it mentally as far as taking Cliff's place, living up to all the people in the family and all the crew people and all. There were forty or forty five people tried out and they wanted to find someone that could take it in all aspects, ya know. They had a million people that could go veroumarrarr and all that shit, but that's only part of it, actually."[cxlix]

There were more changes in the band as they decided to move from a practice space in El Cerrito which they humourously named 'The Metalli-Mansion' to a house between adjacent towns Berkeley and Albany which had previously been rented by sound engineer Mark Whitaker. The band would eventually settle in Marin County, north of San Francisco. Cliff was no longer here, but Metallica was not finished.

... And Justice For All
1988-1989

"There's a lot of things people have totally forgotten about, they're so caught up in this... Looking good, being seen in the right places, playing the fucking game. I get real sick of that shit. That has nothing to do with real life, with being alive."

James Hetfield[cl]

Hair and glam metal which had dominated the Sunset Strip in Los Angeles, the City Of Angels, was the antithesis of what Metallica were about; then along came an LA band called Guns N' Roses. They were the new kids on the block and made Mötley Crüe look frivolous by comparison. Guns N' Roses (Gunners) were punk, hard rock and metal all rolled into one and looked totally unlike any other band. Fronted by the famously tempestuous singer Axl Rose, their 1987 debut *Appetite For Destruction* is now hailed as one of the most important albums in the annals of rock and is also the biggest-selling debut album in American popular music history.

This pivotal moment in rock's canon features the classic line-up of the band: singer Axl Rose, guitarist Slash, bassist Duff McKagan, rhythm guitarist Izzy Stradlin and drummer Steven Adler. Seemingly overnight, many of the LA bands looked outdated compared to Gunners who were as controversial as the Rolling Stones in their 1960s heyday (Metallica would tour with Gunners on the manic Guns N' Roses/Metallica Stadium Tour in 1992). Everything surrounding Guns N' Roses was about excess. Period.

The three bands that had made up the Big Four of thrash with Metallica were also busy: Megadeth were set to release 1988's *So Far, So Good... So What!*; Slayer were about to release the follow-up to their masterpiece *Reign In Blood* with 1988's *South Of*

Heaven; and Anthrax had released 1987's *Among The Living* and would release *State Of Euphoria* the following year.

The Big Four had reached towering heights of success and become flag-bearers for the genre, informing the rest of the world that American metal was a force to be reckoned with. Mainstream hard rock acts like Van Halen were also making dents in the charts while seasoned artists such as Alice Cooper (*Constrictor*) and Aerosmith (*Permanent Vacation*) enjoyed notable comebacks. By contrast British metal seemed like a relic from the past. Yet whereas the aforementioned US rock bands certainly sounded American, the metal bands were distinctly European in many ways. "We pretty much grew up in public... We started when we were like nineteen, twenty years old. And our whole adult life has been spent living, eating, shitting, breathing Metallica," commented Kirk Hammett on their dedication to the metal cause.[cli]

Following the North American and European legs with the late Cliff Burton, the final leg of the Damage, Inc. Tour consisted of world dates and this is when James Newsted was introduced to Metallica's metal crazy fans. Newsted had played his first gigs in the band at the Country Club in Reseda, CA and on the following night at Jezebel's in Anaheim.

The world tour lasted from September 8, 1987 to February 13, 1988 and included the band's first visit to Japan for five sold out shows in November. Looking back at Metallica's first experience in that country, Lars Ulrich said in 1989 (during the band's second visit): "We went out there and done our shit and they just sat there through the whole show and clapping politely, and we thought, 'What the fuck is going on here?!' We thought they didn't like it or something, but then you talk to them after the show and you find out that it's like the best gig they've seen in their life! So they have a really different way of showing emotion up here, they're just so subdued, but after a while you realise that they're into it as much as the kids in Bradford or Dallas, Texas or wherever."[clii]

In the United States, Metallica was supported by Metal Church. However, during the following month after the tour,

James Hetfield broke his wrist (again) during another skateboarding accident. The famed artist Pushead (aka Brian Schroeder) said: "It was their first time skating an empty pool – James was really excited and asked me a lot of questions. I showed him some lines, and soon he was ripping it up – he was hitting tiles and going for coping. Then it happened. James somehow lost his balance coming down off the transition into the flat around the drain and fell backward. His wrist snapped and the bone was protruding out from his wrist brace. That basically ended James' skating career, since it affected his main career."[cliii] The first Metallica skateboard design was done in 1986 – the 'Pirate'.

As a result, a planned performance on *Saturday Night Live* was consequently cancelled. Almost it seemed as a kind of therapy after the death of Cliff Burton but also to welcome Newsted into the band and test out their new rehearsal space, the band then released the covers collection *The $5.98 EP: Garage Days Revisited* in August, which they'd mostly recorded at the Conway in LA. Kirk Hammett commented: "Our older covers definitely have a certain rough charm because we didn't put them under a microscope or record them as anally as we would normally record our own songs."[cliv]

The covers were largely recorded at Ulrich's garage but later re-recorded when the band bought a new studio. This now ultra-rare collector's item features the following tracks: 'Helpless' (Diamond Head), 'The Small Hours' (Holocaust), 'The Wait' (Killing Joke), 'Crash Course In Brain Surgery' (Budgie) and 'Last Caress/Green Hell' (Misfits). The EP peaked at Number 27 in the UK. (It is now out of print but those cover versions along with some others were included on the 1998 double CD set, *Garage Inc.*)

Lars Ulrich: "It's definitely easier to work with other people's material. We like to turn them into something very Metallica, different than how the original artist did it. You don't get so fucking anal about it, and you can bang these covers out in like five minutes."[clv]

"Cover songs are a part of our history, and fans know that," he continued. "We have just put them all in a nice little package for easy listening... We don't sit and analyse things on a sales level... there are people who'll get off on hearing what we do to a Thin Lizzy track."[clvi]

As mentioned, there were various reasons behind the recording of *The $5.98 EP: Garage Days Revisited*. Kirk Hammett explained: "Doing that album was also a good way for us to break Jason in to the public and give our audience a preview of what was to come. We needed to buy some time, because we really weren't ready to record another full-length album yet. We didn't have anything new written. So it was a good way for us to put some product out there and take our time before getting ready..."[clvii]

They also released *Cliff 'Em All*, a video collection in memory of the deceased bassist. The title of the VHS collection is an obvious homage to Metallica's classic debut album, *Kill 'Em All*. The collection consists of bootleg videos, TV appearances and some professional footage of Burton's three and a half years in Metallica. Metal anoraks were also pleased to see footage of Dave Mustaine's stint in Metallica too, shot on March 19, 1983 shortly before he was ousted from the band. The video contains performances of: 'Creeping Death', 'Am I Evil?', 'Damage, Inc.', 'Master Of Puppets', '(Anesthesia) Pulling Teeth', 'Whiplash', 'The Four Horsemen', 'Fade To Black', 'Seek & Destroy', 'Welcome Home (Sanitarium)', 'For Whom The Bell Tolls', 'No Remorse' and 'Metal Militia'. There's some footage of one of Burton's famed bass solos while there are also narrations from Ulrich, Hetfield and Hammett. The rare VHS gives fans an interesting glimpse into the inner world of Metallica during the early Cliff Burton years.

On August 20, Metallica played a warm-up gig at the famed London venue 100 Club and then from August 22 to August 30 they toured Europe as part of the Monsters Of Rock Festival Tour, although the 'tour' actually included only three shows: they returned to England on August 22 to perform for the second time at the rock stronghold of Castle Donington and thereafter they played two shows in West Germany. The Donington Festival was headlined by Bon Jovi with Metallica third on the bill under

Dio. The other acts included Anthrax, W.A.S.P. and Cinderella. During the tour, their regular set-list looked like this: 'Creeping Death', 'For Whom The Bell Tolls', 'Fade To Black', 'Leper Messiah', 'Welcome Home (Sanitarium)', 'Seek & Destroy', 'Master Of Puppets', 'Whiplash', 'Am I Evil?' and 'Battery'. Metallica were not too impressed with their Donington performance as it was the first time (discounting the 100 Club gig in London) that they'd played live in several months.

Broadcasters and presenters The Baileys Brothers (Mick and Dez) were there to introduce the bands. Dez Bailey recalls, "The 1987 Monsters of Rock saw a divide between rock fans as they were those who wanted their music fast, hard and heavy as in Metallica and those who wanted it glam and commercial (Cinderella and Bon Jovi). I think if the Bailey Brothers hadn't walked out on stage and pulled the audience together there would have been trouble for sure. As for hanging with Metallica, well, we had already seen what the guys were capable of in Germany when we were on the bill with them at the Lorely Festival and interviewed many of the acts for Sky [TV] but by the time the MOR came around they were huge. Our memory of them playing there was awesome and we probably witnessed one of the best metal acts since Judas Priest, the intense power and musicianship put them in another zone. Metallica were a movement, an arrow-head that said, 'Fuck your glam and pop rock, move over or we will kick your ass!' We were more concerned with making sure the fans had some cool music throughout the day than hanging with the bands, we could do that at the after-show party, yeah, the usual [club DJ] norm was to stick a tape on and piss off to the bar and leave the fans to it but we changed that mind-set and at least gave the fans some respect."[clviii]

The band ended 1987 with some rehearsals as they were planning ideas for their fourth album. In many respects this next record would be a pivotal album in the early years of Metallica's career because not only was it the first not to feature Cliff Burton but they also had a lot to live up to after the critical success of *Kill 'Em All*, *Ride The Lightning* and *Master Of Puppets*.

On January 28, 1988, Metallica entered the One On One Recording Studios in Los Angeles to begin work on what was to be the first album to feature James Newsted. They have always been very particular about their choice of recording studio, paying exacting attention to detail on such issues as the size of the control room and recording suites. The band had enjoyed working at Sweet Silence Studios in Copenhagen where they recorded *Ride The Lightning* and *Master Of Puppets*. In Europe – as opposed to the United States – the studios generally have in-house engineers, which is how they met Flemming Rasmussen who produced the latter two albums and the band had been impressed with his work with the English rock band Rainbow (founded by former Deep Purple guitarist Ritchie Blackmore) on their 1983 opus *Difficult To Cure*. For the fourth release, Metallica's record company had set up a tour of LA's recording studios and had Hetfield choose one suitable for the band's needs.

"This time around we didn't want to make any recording decisions until we had all the songs written," explained Ulrich. "So we started writing in October and it only took eight or nine weeks to write the songs. It went a lot quicker than we thought it would."[clix]

The latest Metallica recruit spoke to Cliff Burton biographer Joel McIver two decades after the album's release. Newsted said: "All the recording I'd done up until that point, including the *Garage Days* EP, was done in a couple of days. That was how I knew to record, right? That's what I knew. So I went in on *Justice*, and obviously there's still weird feelings going on. It was the first time we'd been in the studio for a real Metallica album, and Cliff's not there."[clx]

It's interesting to learn the origins of the songs that made the final cut. "A lot of the songs that were written for *...And Justice For All* were written on the *Master Of Puppets* tour when Cliff was still in the band and stuff," commented Newsted in 1989. "We get all our tapes together and whoever comes up with the coolest shit, that's obviously the stuff we're going to use, whatever is the most appealing stuff, and James comes up with some pretty sick shit ya know, and so does Kirk, so it's just a matter, it's just up to me to write cooler stuff than them. It comes down to, we just use whatever is the very best, 'cause we have ideas for days, but just, you have to, ya know, sift through them or whatever and figure out what's best."[clxi]

Hetfield and Ulrich spoke to journalist Richard Gehr in 1988 about the band's riffs, for example how they create riffs on the road and archive them for future use. Hetfield said: "Like, some shit is strong enough to be the main idea of a tune. Then we go through the tapes and try to find possible bridges, choruses, middle bits or whatever. After we have the skeleton of a song, we start getting a feel for what the song's really like. Then we search for a title from a list of titles that fits with the riffing's mood."[clxii]

The band opted to work with Mike Clink who had made a huge name for himself with Guns N' Roses' debut album *Appetite For Destruction*. However, the relationship between Clink and Metallica was to be short-lived and after two months Rasmussen entered the picture once he was free of his other production duties (Clink was credited with engineering the drums on 'The Shortest Straw' and 'Harvester Of Sorrow' and for the recording two cover versions, 'Breadfan' and 'The Prince' which were initially used as B-sides on the single 'Harvester Of Sorrow' and were later used on the double CD *Garage Inc.*). Ulrich explained: "Mike did a fine job and did us all a big favour by coming into the studio and helping us out, but Flemming is the only one who can record Metallica..."[clxiii]

Kirk Hammett: "We're the master procrastinators. We tend to work eighty percent of the time on the first ten percent of the album and spend the other twenty percent of the time on the last ninety percent of the record. We tend to sweat and toil on the beginning of a record, and a lot of that has to do with establishing a stride that works for us. And sometimes establishing that momentum is very difficult."[clxiv]

Newsted was a obviously something of an outsider and it wasn't easy for him to fit into the band and join in on the rock 'n' roll camaraderie when he was recording his bass parts during the day with Rasmussen while the rest of the band often worked at night. Was he treated badly from the get-go? Metallica biographer Joel McIver comments, "Not as badly as people think. They took the piss out of him for a while, but he ended up with a vast fortune and he was a tough kid, so don't feel too sorry for him."[clxv]

Newsted explained at length his memories of recording his bass for the band's fourth opus to Joel McIver: "I stepped in with an assistant engineer and I had my same gear that I would just play on the stage. There was no time taken about, 'You place this microphone here, and this one will sound better than that... should we mix it with the DI? Should we use this bass instead of that bass? Should we get that tonality? Should you use a pick? Should you use your fingers? Any of the things that I know now, that make a really good bass sound. You plug in, you play the song. I could play those songs standing on my head with my eyes closed, any of those songs. I rehearsed those up the ass. Right?"[clxvi]

Ulrich and Hetfield were certainly the dominant force in the studio, making the most decisions and having full control over the music. "Lars and I were (sic) clamped down pretty hard on a lot of the stuff in the past and we could see the other guys were a little unhappy," confessed Hetfield. "Everyone's gotta be happy so you've gotta give..."[clxvii]

Lars Ulrich: "One thing I think we went for this time around when we were mixing the album is a very up-front, in-your-face type sound. We approached it in a way that was very similar to the *$5.98* EP, in the sense that we wanted all the instruments to practically jump out of the speakers and slap you in the face while you're listening to it."[clxviii]

They came out of the studio on May 1, 1988. The fourth album deserves further examination as it remains a controversial release in the band's back-catalogue. In the 1980s it was felt that the synthesiser was going to replace the guitar with bands like ZZ Top and even Judas Priest experimenting with new sounds and including that instrument in their latest recordings. It was a popular choice with progressive rock bands and even AOR and melodic rock outfits too who used it to boost their sound to create moments of pomp and bombast. Bands like Journey and Foreigner used synths regularly but it was a no-go area for

Metallica. Kirk Hammett: "It makes no sense for us to be on the cutting edge of it, finding the newest samples and tools and all that stuff because we thrive on a classic formula that in my opinion will never die, and that is good ol' hard rock and heavy metal. But we're constantly looking for things that will open our sound up more, that's just us. But before anyone asks, no, it won't be electronic."[clxix]

The band's fourth album was certainly less melodic than its predecessors; more direct and forceful, cold yet intricate. "We never would have written guitar harmonies or instrumentals or songs with very intricate melodies and orchestrations without Cliff," said Hetfield years later.[clxx] It was Burton who gave the band's music more focus and depth and perhaps explains the distant and almost sterile sound of *…And Justice For All.* The album would have sounded much different had Burton been alive.

Does *…And Justice For All* sound so different from its three predecessors because Burton was not involved? Cliff Burton biographer Joel McIver says, "Possibly, the mix would have been different if Cliff had been in charge of it as well as James and Lars, but we'll never know."[clxxi]

When asked the same question, metal writer and fan Bob Nalbandian comments, "In a way yes, but… since Lars and James were the main songwriters I don't think *Justice* would have differed a whole lot if Cliff were alive and still in the band at that point. I think the latter albums would likely have been a lot different if Cliff was still around for those recordings."[clxxii]

The recordings represent the band's train of thought at that point in time and showed a degree of complexity and anger. Diamond Head (still) had a fundamental impact on the songs that feature on the band's fourth studio opus. James Hetfield explained years later: "You can really hear their impact on *…And Justice for All* which was where we really started to go over the top with that type of songwriting. Sometimes we look back at a lot of our material and wonder how – or why – we ever came up with certain parts. Or wonder why we just didn't turn certain riffs into their own songs, because they were so good."[clxxiii]

Many fans noticed the double-bass drum sound on the song 'One' for example. Ulrich was certainly one of the leading pioneers of the thrash metal drum beats and just as he'd proven with 'Metal Militia' (*Kill 'Em All*), 'Fight Fire With Fire' (*Ride The Lightning*) and 'Battery' (*Master Of Puppets),* with the *...And Justice For All* track 'Dyers Eve' Ulrich became one of metal's most distinctive drummers. His style of drumming was fast, fierce and aggressive, often with simplified drum beats and a double bass technique which many metal drummers adopted in the 1980s and subsequent decades.

"Bands who take the metal in different directions – like those who incorporate tribal rhythms, samplers, and sequencers into their tunes – will always get great respect from me," commented James Newsted. "You have to keep exploring and going forward."[clxxiv]

Hammett was more than comfortable using his iconic Gibson Flying V which he bought because German guitarist Michael Schenker had one and it gave his playing a much bigger and heavier sound. Hammett had used it on Metallica's previous three albums too.

Though *...And Justice For All* is not a concept album per se, there are consistent themes rippling throughout the nine lengthy tracks. Perhaps inspired by futuristic novels like George Orwell's *1984*, the themes present in the album include political, legal and social injustice in a world of censorship, war and nuclear weapons.

Metallica had become so popular with a generation of kids that they could write and say what they wanted to, but sometimes kids would take it literally. "All these freak people are trying to build in this huge symbolism between the music they listen to and the lyrics and why they did this..." James Hetfield commented before the release of *...And Justice For All.* "The lyrics I write, I write pretty much for myself. I'm not telling people how to think. Like, 'If you don't believe the way I do then you're not a real Metallica fan,' or some shit like that."[clxxv]

With each successive album the band was entering dark territory, lyrically, as Hetfield later attested: "All those things I say that you think are sarcasm – well, I'm not kidding... I thought it was supposed to be simple so that it sounds like some kid in his garage just trying to do his best."[clxxvi]

Metal bands often write about the world's social ills in their lyrics and contrary to popular belief these bands and their fans are some of the most literate of music lovers, regardless of genre boundaries. Lars explained at the time: "This new one has a general theme – definitely staying away from the word 'concept' – running through it which is based on the whole justice thing. We thought that it would make a strong album title, so we decided to use it."[clxxvii]

The one thing Metallica did stay away from was the occult, which had been tried and tested with bands from the early beginnings of metal with Black Sabbath to the theatrically blood-thirsty NWOBHM band Venom to the tongue-in-cheek lyrics and imagery of Iron Maiden. It just wasn't Metallica's cup of tea. Metallica were never about creating fantasy worlds within their lyrics like Ronnie James Dio and Manowar; their lyrics reflected the anger and angst of a young generation of kids that probably had more in common with the punk bands of the 1970s. This meant that Metallica's lyrics would, in many ways, endure far more than other metal band of their ilk because there'd always be a generation of angry young men. They documented where they were at that point in time so each album serves as a precise and personal historical document.

Heavy metal has been perceived by some as a sexist genre due in the main to bands like Mötley Crüe but Metallica had stayed away from such ills. "Well, I've never even thought about it like that," said Newsted. "We've never been a band that sang about anything that had to do with anybody being one sex or another. James' lyrics have always been an open thing to whoever it was that was listening to it, whether you were a man or a woman or otherwise. That's just the way it is. We never sang about fast cars or doing girls. Metallica has a lot more to say than that."[clxxviii]

Ulrich had long since been the band's spokesman but Hetfield was the one fans idolised and recognised the most. Of course, he is not only the band's frontman but also the chief lyricist. James Newsted said over a decade later: "He will not be denied. You can

burn him, break him or whatever and he'll come back and kick your ass. And I still believe that. He's still my hero and still someone I look up to greatly and he won't be beaten. You have to know that."[clxxix]

Although Metallica were very busy mixing the new album they did take time out to play some live shows. On May 23 and

24 they played two warm-up gigs at The Troubadour in Los Angeles and from May 27 to July 30 they performed as part of the Monsters Of Rock Festival Tour of the United States with headliners Van Halen and the Scorpions, Dokken and Kingdom Come. "The biggest surprise has definitely been the Van Halen guys," enthused Lars Ulrich. "You would think that a band like them, after something like twelve years together or something like that, would have an attitude problem or wouldn't have their feet planted on the ground, but the Van Halen guys are definitely some of the most 'down-to-earth' people you could ever meet."[clxxx]

Metallica performed in front of audiences of over 50,000 (despite some cancelled shows) and it certainly helped raise their fan-base. Metallica were second from the bottom after Kingdom Come with a sixty minute set consisting of: 'Creeping Death', 'For Whom The Bell Tolls', 'Welcome Home (Sanitarium)', 'Harvester Of Sorrow', 'Whiplash', 'Fade To Black', 'Seek & Destroy', 'Master Of Puppets', the Misfits track 'Last Caress', 'Am I Evil?' and 'Battery'.

Brian Rademacher, former *Metal Forces* staff photographer and founder of the acclaimed rock site, *Rock Eyez*, recalls, "It was June 11, 1988 at JFK Stadium in Philadelphia on the Monsters Of Rock Tour with Van Halen headlining with Metallica, the Scorpions, Dokken and Kingdom Come. I was thirty years old at the time and working a night job and also a staff photographer for the mighty *Metal Forces* magazine from the UK. The Monsters Of Rock Tour was my first outdoor concert to photograph so I wasn't sure what I was in for. As I got my press/photo pass and was escorted to the stage grounds and looked up at this monstrous metal scaffolding with a wooden plank at the top and the security guards saying that is where photographers are shooting from, I said to myself 'Holy shit!' [because] I wasn't a weightless skinny kid and wasn't sure I was going to make it to the top. I really wanted to shoot Metallica so I did my best and you can see my results by the front cover of this book. I went on to shoot some of the best metal acts in the world like Megadeth, KISS, W.A.S.P., and many others…"[clxxxi]

In terms of Hetfield's well-documented drinking, this was without doubt a very indulgent tour. Hetfield confessed: "That was the Jagermeister days. I am still hearing stories about it, like that I slugged Lars but I don't remember any of it. We were drunk the whole time. We were very much into drinking and having a good fucking time. That was the pinnacle of all the debauchery, drinking, fucking and general insanity."[clxxxii]

James Newsted affirmed: "I think that one thing that really needs to be cleared up, that I'm not sure how it's been misconstrued, is that the other addictions have nothing to do with substances. As long as I have known him, he has never touched anything other than alcohol. I know for a fact that he's never done any kind of amphetamines, cocaine or anything like that in his life ever. I know he's never done LSD or ecstasy or any of that shit ever. Any of that thing that people think has to do with drugs is completely wrong. As far as the alcoholism thing, he's always liked to drink. Think about it, it's fucking Metallica. Alcoholica, that was us, that's what we do. That's part of the lifestyle..."[clxxxiii]

In between shows, Ulrich and Hetfield had to fly back and forth to Bearsville in New York where they were mixing *...And Justice For All* with Steve Thompson and Michael Barbiero. It proved very tiring for the Metallica duo. "Yes, it was starting to really piss us off there towards the end of the mixing sessions," Ulrich told *Metal Forces'* Borivoj Krgin about juggling the mixing duties with touring. "The last couple of weeks were probably the most hectic two weeks in the band's existence."[clxxxiv]

Newsted had never even met Thompson or Barbiero, who had previously worked with a variety of recording artists such as Whitney Houston, Madonna, the Rolling Stones, Prince, Cinderella, Tesla and Guns N' Roses. Newsted told British metal author Joel McIver: "I was so in the dirt! I was so disappointed when I heard the final mix – I basically blocked it out, like people do with shit. We were firing on all cylinders, and shit was happening. I was just rolling with it and going forward. What was I gonna do? Say, 'We gotta go remix it!' when we were down to the last minutes with people saying, 'We gotta say when, we gotta say when!'"[clxxxv]

On the other hand, James Hetfield explained: "I think the problem with a lot of people who specialise in mixing is they set up the mix the way they're used to mixing bands, and everyone ends up sounding like those mixes. What's great about these guys is they go out of their way to keep the band's identity completely together."[clxxxvi]

"Everything's way up front and there's not a lot of 'verb or echo," he continued to tell journalist Richard Gehr. "We really went out of our way to make sure that what we put on the tape was what we wanted, so the mixing procedure would be as easy as possible and not like the old saying, 'We'll save it in the mix.'"[clxxxvii]

...And Justice For All opens with the six minute long 'Blackened' which was bassist Jason Newsted's first co-songwriting credit on a Metallica album; the lyrics deal with the end of the world and indeed the end of humanity. It's a musically powerful song with muscular guitars but the drums are too pronounced and there's a need for a stronger bass line though it does have a progressive tint as it goes from one extreme to another. It remains one of the album's most popular songs amongst fans. '...And Justice For All' is an epic metal track that has caused a split in the Metallica fanbase with some fans believing it is far too long. There are also lots of changes in tempo but the song lacks more distinctive riffs. There are some drum beats that sound different from Ulrich's regular drum sound. The lyrics are about social injustice and quotes the American Pledge Of Allegiance. 'Eye Of The Beholder' opens with some sturdy riffs and although the tempo is slower than its siblings, the riffs have a more pronounced stomp. It's a fairly complex song, musically, and one of the album's lead tracks in terms of quality, with a lot of groove. The song's lyrics concern the limitations of freedom of speech. 'One' opens with some slow and clean guitars before it becomes progressive; heavier and faster with thrash metal guitars. There are sound effects at the start of the song which add to its central theme about war (based upon the 1939 novel *Johnny Got His Gun* by Dalton Trumbo). 'The Shortest

Straw' stands at just over six minutes long and is one of the album's least well-known songs but it has some sturdy riffs and a memorable guitar solo. Lyrically, the song deals with the 1950s Communist Blacklisting that took place in Hollywood and all over the United States. 'Harvester Of Sorrow' is an angry song to match the subject matter about a man who goes crazy and takes his anger out on his family and the listener is left to assume he killed them. This is another track on the opus that has a strong progressive texture to it and there are some standout moments of instrumentation and layers of guitars.

'The Frayed Ends Of Sanity' is a fast-moving track with some intricate guitar work and indelible song lines. 'To Live Is To Die' is the longest song on the album and was written as a tribute to late bassist Cliff as the song title was apparently a phrase Burton was keen on. It was the last Metallica song to feature a co-writing credit by Burton. Burton had written the song's bass riffs before he died but they had not yet been used so Newsted played the song's bass parts. It's an almost fully instrumental track with some really powerful moments and is the only instrumental which Newsted played on. Lars Ulrich explained to *Metal Forces'* Borivoj Krgin in 1988: "A lot of people might give us flak about this one because it features riffs written by Cliff [Burton] a few months before he was killed just like they gave us flak for using Dave Mustaine's stuff… but the truth of the matter is, these riffs were just so huge and so Metallica-sounding that we had to use them. We're certainly not trying to dwell on Cliff's death or anything like that… we're simply using the best ideas we had available, and this is one of them."[clxxxviii]

The closing track is 'Dyers Eve' which is a rapid-firing thrash metal onslaught with some killer guitar work and angst-ridden vocals. The lyrics are rather morbid about a child who has been hidden from the real world by his parents, kept a prisoner in his home and so he thinks about suicide.

…And Justice For All doesn't quite have the same power, the same guttural kick as its three predecessors but it does have some profound moments, and some snippets of absolute metal genius. The songs are not quite as engaging as those on *Master Of Puppets*

but having said that much of the guitar work is exemplary. The production is clinical and cold and though it remains Metallica's most progressive album, there are obvious flaws present. "Love it," says Metallica biographer Joel McIver. "It needs a remix but the original tinny sound does have a certain charm."[clxxxix]

Bob Nalbandian: "Didn't like it [*Justice*] as much. I thought *Master* was a much stronger album. I didn't really care for the production of *Justice*, way too dry sounding, and also thought the songs were too long and drawn out."[cxcm]

With ...*And Justice For All* there was indeed a drastic change in sound which many fans noticed from the get-go. Some fans had immediately complained that Newsted's bass had been toned down, Ulrich's drums sounded different and some felt the production was somewhat weaker than the first three albums. James Newsted made a comment about his contributions to the album years later: "I was on *Justice*, almost... and they actually gave me a songwriting credit on 'My Friend Of Misery', which I think is a pretty cool song..."[cxci]

There were reasons behind the obvious lack of bass on their latest album. "There was a lot of grief and a lot of anguish when Cliff died, and basically Jason was the punching bag," Hammett said. "We vented so much on Jason because of the whole bus accident and Cliff's death, and it really wasn't fair to do that to him."[cxcii]

Had Cliff Burton been alive the bass guitars would have sounded drastically different. They would have been far more audible for one thing. What was the difference between Cliff Burton's bass and James Newsted's? Lars Ulrich: "The main different between Jason's and Cliff's writing is that Jason tends to write a lot more with the guitar in mind whereas Cliff's stuff was always like really weird and off-the-wall. If anything, I think Jason's stuff is a lot closer to James' and my songwriting than Cliff's shit ever was."[cxciii]

However, even though Newsted had some of his own ideas for songwriting not all of them were used and some reports suggested he was not too happy about that. Nevertheless the band did use his lyrics for 'Blackened'.

...*And Justice For All* was released in August 1988 and was the band's first Top 10 hit in the USA, reaching Number 6. Whatever criticisms that were aimed at the album clearly had no affect on its sales. It did great for the band in the UK too, peaking at Number 4. 'Harvester Of Sorrow' was a hit single in the UK reaching Number 20 and 'Eye Of The Beholder' reached Number 27. The band also released '...And Justice For All' as a single. With a hit album under their belts, had Metallica now become a mainstream band?

Fans had waited two and a half years since *Master Of Puppets* and some felt it was too long but the band had had a lot to deal with: they'd committed themselves to an eleven month world tour, they'd released an EP and VHS tape and also had to deal with the death of Cliff Burton and James Hetfield's skateboarding accident. They were not sitting around idly. Metallica were fortunate enough to have control over their music; they were effectively self-employed and ran their own business.

Metal Forces co-founder and editor Bernard Doe says, "*Master Of Puppets* was always going to be a hard album to top, but for me ...*And Justice For All* was still a disappointment at the time, apart from 'One' of course which is arguably up there as one of Metallica's finest moments. I also found the production rather limp-wristed. Far less accessible than previous releases, much of the material from the album was quickly dropped from the band's live set or stripped down and relegated to the '...And Justice For All Medley', which spoke volumes at the time."[cxciv]

By contrast, critical opinion was mostly very positive with rave reviews in *Kerrang!* and *Metal Hammer*. Upon the album's original release, Michael Azerrad wrote in *Rolling Stone:* "Thrash is too demeaning a term for this 'metametal', a marvel of precisely channeled aggression. There are few verse-chorus structures, just collages done at Mach 8. The album is crammed with diatribes about nuclear winter, the right to die and judicial corruption, delivered in an aggressive bark by rhythm guitarist James Hetfield."

Azerrad reviewed ...*And Justice For All* with Bon Jovi's *New*

Jersey (also released in 1988) and concluded his review by saying, "Bon Jovi's trick is to use heavy-metal chords and still sound absolutely safe. Rock 'n' roll used to be rebellion disguised as commercialism; now so much of it is commercialism disguised as rebellion. Bon Jovi is safe as milk; Metallica harks back to the time when rock's bite was worse than its bark."

The famed American rock critic Robert Christgau gave the album a rating of C+ in his historic *Consumer Guide Reviews* and merely said: "Problem isn't that it's more self-conscious than *Master Of Puppets*, which is inevitable when your stock in trade is compositions not songs. Problem is that it goes on longer – which is also inevitable when your stock in trade is compositions not songs. Just ask Yes."

When asked why the first four albums are an important part of not only Metallica's career but the entire metal genre, photographer Bill Hale, says, "I would say the first three albums (never heard the fourth). The fans over here [California] wanted/needed to have a band all their own. Yeah, we all dug Motörhead, Diamond Head, Maiden, Angel Witch but they were not one of us. Metallica was!"[cxcv]

In time, the album would continue to receive adulation. Here's what the rock and metal scribes said in the noughties: Steve Huey's astute review at *MSN Music* said: "The most immediately noticeable aspect of *...And Justice For All* isn't Metallica's still-growing compositional sophistication or the apocalyptic lyrical portrait of a society in decay. It's the weird, bone-dry production. The guitars buzz thinly, the drums click more than pound, and Jason Newsted's bass is nearly inaudible."

He continued: "It's a shame that the cold, flat sound obscures some of the sonic details, because *...And Justice For All* is Metallica's most complex, ambitious work; every song is an expanded suite, with only two of the nine tracks clocking in at under six minutes."

Punk News stated: "*Justice* contains Metallica's most sophisticated, heaviest riffs yet. A lot of changing tempos, a lot of weird rhythms, a lot of palm-muted guitars and a lot of excellent solos courtesy of one Kirk Hammett, specifically 'One',

'Blackened' and 'Dyers Eve'. What's interesting about this record is how most of its solos are actually divided in two, with a small break in between."

Sputnikmusic enthused: "Overall this album has a very angst feel. No, this is not for anyone who watches *Alley Mcbeal* [*sic*]. The lyrics are violent, the riffs are fast, it truly makes you want to kick some ass. To be more specific a lot of lyrics were pretty much insulting our country's leaders. You can hear and really feel the aggression in James' vocals as they flow through the speakers."

Martin Popoff – the Canadian metal historian and author – gives the author his opinion of *...And Justice For All*: "My views on this album aren't all that innovative or different from anybody else's. One thing I do remember though, I definitely didn't draw as much value out of this album [as] I did the previous two. I love the fact it was proggy and anti-commercial; I didn't even have complaints with the production job. It was just kind of cool hearing a very extreme, obscure production job, when there was so much wetness on hair metal albums, although don't get me wrong, I totally dug most of those hair metal bands as well, hating only Bon Jovi, Poison and Cinderella, really. But yeah, everybody complained about the production, they complained about the long songs, and yes, truth be told, it was a little extreme. Metallica on this record evoked that same reservation I had with the first record, where everybody crouched around and paid homage to riff. Only this time, there was less logic to it. Whereas on *Kill 'Em All*, you felt that there were two or three perfectly fine riffs stuck together, forced to live together, and presto, here's our song; with *Justice*, there were more like fourteen riffs per song, and still, they didn't all necessarily have to be there, or all necessarily work with each other, intro upon intro. So yeah, I suppose this album is the band's *Sin After Sin*, or their *Far Beyond Driven*, which is perfectly admirable, although like I say, it's a cool, intellectual album, and not so much one for the heart, like the previous two."[cxcvi]

Despite the conflicting opinions on the record, the legacy of *...And Justice For All* (like its three predecessors) is assured and though many claim the band's fourth album to be a flawed masterpiece it is a significant record in Metallica's mighty arsenal of studio opuses. It was awarded Platinum status in the United States twelve times and remains a popular metal album; since 1991 alone it has sold over five million copies. 'One' was ranked at Number 7 in the '100 Greatest Guitar Solos Of All Time' by *Guitar World* while *IGN Music* placed the album at Number 9 in the list of 'The Top 25 Metal Albums' and it is also featured in the reference tome *1001 Albums You Must Hear Before You Die*.

In time, members of Metallica would later re-evaluate their opinion about *...And Justice For All*. "I must admit that listening to *Justice* now, I do wonder why we put three minute intros onto some of the stuff," Ulrich commented in 1990. "Obviously that's what we were into at the time, but right now, I'm more into the songwriting style we had on *Ride The Lightning*. I also know a lot of people found *Justice* difficult to get into but I'm not gonna sit here and apologise for that. I mean, out of all the Metallica albums to date, it's no secret that *Justice* is by far the less accessible of them all, I just find it funny that it's sold better than the others by over three to one..."[cxcvii]

James Hetfield confessed almost a decade later: "[... *And Justice For All*] was really, really anal. Every little bit was worked out. The arrangement was so orchestrated that it got really stiff, and when we were on tour it got really boring. So we knew we had to move on."[cxcviii]

This was the period when Metallica really began to challenge themselves and their fans; many of whom would not welcome Metallica's enthusiasm for new sounds. Hetfield explained the band's musical landscape a decade later: "We were always trying to write such epic style pieces, especially on [...*And*] *Justice For All*, our pieces were really long and took you through these whole long mazes of sounds."[cxcix]

Indeed, due to the length of the songs many of them are rarely – if ever – played live. Every song lasts over five minutes with the longest being 'To Live Is To Die' clocking in at nine minutes and 48 seconds. They purportedly stopped playing the title-track because of the length (9:44) and the response it got from audiences but 'One', 'Blackened' and 'Harvester Of Sorrow' have been played regularly in more recent years on the live front.

It remains an album that has split the Metallica fanbase with its fair amount of fans and critics. Nonetheless, it's certainly an important record in the Metallica cannon. Not only was it the first album not to feature Cliff Burton but it was – in hindsight – the end of an era for the band as they would enter the new decade with different ideas. Metal had changed and Metallica were going to change.

To promote their fourth album, Metallica kicked off the Damaged Justice Tour on September 11, 1988 which would take them right through the winter. The Damaged Justice Tour was the fourth headlining tour by Metallica following the *Kill 'Em All* For One, Bang That Head That Doesn't Bang, *Ride The Lightning* and Damage, Inc. Tours. The European leg ran from September 11 to November 5, 1988, followed by a huge trek across the rest of the world which ran from November 15 to October 8 of the following year.

Exciter's John Ricci remembers seeing the band in concert in his home town of Ottawa, Canada: "They played a huge arena where they had a dynamic stage show which was a far departure from the time at the Marquee Club [in London, 1984]. Again they performed an over the top show and the crowd went wild."[cc]

As Metallica were getting older and their fanbase was growing up with them, would there arrive a point when they couldn't

manage to sustain such high levels of energy on stage anymore?

Lars Ulrich: "I'm not intimidated by it. Because no matter what, we still go out and play, and we still fire up in the same way. When you're eighteen or nineteen years-old, you have that gang mentality in your band. It's this tiny little situation. Nobody can stray outside of it. It's the thing you do when you're eighteen, nineteen, twenty. And that's ten, twelve years ago for me."[cci]

Metallica had always maintained a strong and loyal relationship with their fans and even though their latest album was probably the least well received of the four albums released thus far, they still remained tight with their fans. They'd still hang around and talk to fans after a show; it was a tradition. "It's always been there and it's continued to be very important to us," explained Newsted. "We're very conscious of making sure that it happens every night and even on nights off, as it were, when kids line up outside the hotel or maybe find us at a club. Metallica has always gone out of their way to keep the intimacy, to keep the bond there. It's very important to us. We know where the bread and butter is coming from and it's important to us to keep the strength and the loyalty intact."[ccii]

The tour consisted of over 270 shows with around four million people worldwide in attendance. Metallica had become a metal juggernaut. During the 1980s rock concerts had became huge, visually stunning events with all manner of spectacles onstage such as extravagant lighting, pyro, stage props and so forth and bands like Iron Maiden, AC/DC, KISS and Alice Cooper were not only exciting to listen to but exhilarating to watch as well. Cooper was undoubtedly the king of onstage rock theatrics and KISS took it to a higher level with bigger stages, more expensive production values and larger audiences. Of course, this meant bands had to rehearse more and be mindful of their stage antics to avoid injury. It wasn't just about playing music anymore; it was an event – it was theatre of sorts. Since the introduction of video cameras – pioneered by the San Francisco AOR gods Journey – it was possible for those fans at the back of the arena or stadium to feel close to the band; to make the show more intimate.

The theatricality came at a price however as Lars Ulrich

explained: "It all becomes so fucking tethered to the lighting cues and the video cues and the production cues. We talk about that a lot, about not becoming a slave to the stuff that surrounds the music. Sometimes I'll be like, 'Why don't we play this?' And the band's into it, but we hear that the lighting designer needs three days to reprogram the rig. We struggle to find the right balance between music, the spontaneous thing, and the show."[cciii]

They also played in Australia for the first time although they had initially planned to tour Down Under in 1986 after playing in Japan but because of Cliff Burton's death that did not happen. The band took a low-key approach to test the water Down Under but all three gigs were sell-outs and rapturously received. Some reports suggested that there was a riot in Sydney but it just seemed that there were some overzealous fans who wanted to get through the doors before they were actually opened!

The band had initially spoken about returning to Europe for more shows in November, 1989 after visiting Brazil but they were exhausted and the whole tour was perhaps a few weeks too long and they were understandably fatigued. They'd achieved an incredible amount in the years since the release of *Kill 'Em All* in 1983 but perhaps they were pushing themselves too far. As Lars Ulrich explained: "Maybe I go a little overboard sometimes by wanting to play all over the place, and if a couple of other guys pull in the opposite direction then I guess it tends to even itself out in the middle. But really we were in no fit state to come over to Europe in November. I think, if we learnt anything on that tour then it was that we should never do a tour that long again..."[cciv]

James Newsted: "We're going to hibernate for a while. Because this thing ends up being sixteen or seventeen months total and it's continuous. So, we're gonna go home and do the little things that we need to do like drive our trucks and shit like that. You know, things you guys take for granted like going to the grocery store or riding your bike or doing whatever, man, playing with the cats, playing with the dogs, roving in your truck, you know, cool shit like that. I'm gonna shoot some guns, ya know, whatever. We're goina hibernate for a bit then get back to writing."[ccv]

By this point in their career, Metallica were well and truly one of the most awe-inspiring live metal bands. There was simple no question about their onstage prowess. They hit all the right buttons; they knew how to control and empower an audience and received adulation from their metal disciples. They were tighter, well-rehearsed and powerful; an onstage destructive force oozing charisma and talent.

Lars Ulrich: "There's the fact that we go out and play every fuckin' gig in the world. I mean, some of the places we have been and will be playing on this [Damaged Justice] tour are places where they don't get a lot of bands because nobody else fuckin' bothers, but our attitude as a band is that we want to take it out to everybody instead of everybody having to find us."[ccvi]

Metallica learned from their idols such as the premier NWOBHM bands and earlier hard rock heavyweights like Deep Purple and Black Sabbath and thus knew how to build a reputation as an indestructible live band. *Made In Japan* – the legendary Deep Purple live album – had a huge impact on Hetfield and Ulrich as the young friends had sat back and listened in awe, wanting one day to have such a global impact.

Unusually within the music industry, Metallica actually allowed fans to bring tape recorders into some shows to record the band's performance, effectively allowing bootlegs to circulate. It was manager Cliff Burnstein's idea who was inspired by the Grateful Dead, the San Francisco rock band that formed in the Bay Area in 1965. It was only at selected shows providing management could come to an agreement with the promoters.

The band rightly assumed that Metallica fans and metal fans in general were collectors and would buy the band's official products as well. "If we know that there's 200 kids out there taping a show, then it's gonna give us a kick in the ass because it's gonna make sure that we've got it together up there on stage, so, all in all, I think it's a fine situation to be in," explained Ulrich to *Metal Forces*' Bernard Doe in 1989.[ccvii]

James Newsted on Metallica bootlegs: "At one time it was only audio. Now it's audio, video, whatever you want. And there's just so much bootleg stuff happening with Metallica. We're a very collectible type of band. Kids are really into getting every single possible type of thing that they can have. There's just hundreds of bootleg albums and bootleg videos, shirts, everything."[ccviii]

However, the band had no solid plans for an official live album, as Lars explained: "I think live albums are a weird thing. I mean, if you look at other band situations you find that sometimes they surface either when bands have run out of creative ideas or they wanna take a year off, y'know, and as we're not in either of those situations we don't think a live release seems like the next logical step at this point in time."[ccix]

Each night the band changed encores and often flittered with various cover versions or just snippets of other artists' songs, including 'Prowler' by Iron Maiden, 'Helpless' by Diamond Head, 'How Many More Times' by Led Zeppelin and 'Black Night' by Deep Purple. They regularly played the following set-list: 'Blackened', 'For Whom The Bell Tolls', 'Welcome Home (Sanitarium)', 'Harvester Of Sorrow', 'The Four Horsemen', 'The Thing That Should Not Be', 'Master Of Puppets', 'Fade To Black', 'Seek & Destroy', '...And Justice For All', 'One', 'Creeping Death', 'Battery', 'Last Caress' (Misfits), 'Am I Evil?' (Diamond Head), 'Whiplash' and 'Breadfan' (Budgie). There was nothing more that Metallica liked to do than pay homage to their inspirations and perhaps introduce some of the more obscure bands to a younger, wider audience.

As a nod to Pink Floyd's tour for their 1979 classic progressive rock opus *The Wall* (when a titular block of bricks collapsed onstage during a huge climax), Metallica created a female statue of Justice (whom they dubbed Doris) which collapsed into a pile of rubble. Ulrich elaborated: "Most rock bands were trying to outdo each other in theatrics. We felt the *Justice* tour was as far as we could take that."[ccx]

In terms of audiences and fan reaction the band were welcomed differently in various areas around the world. "The South American countries, especially Brazil," commented Hetfield, "they've got some pretty good rhythm. America's the worst, man. They're like faster, faster, faster! You know, that's the lifestyle. If it's faster, it's better."[ccxi]

Around this time Hammett had also picked up another iconic guitar in addition to his Gibson Flying V. "I bought my first Les Paul in 1988," he confessed years later. "I went on to buy another after that in 1989 and then I just started buying Les Paul's on a regular basis. It's mainly because I just love Les Paul's, especially the old ones. The old Les Paul's which had the PAF pickups are just amazing to me."[ccxii]

The five musicians learned how to live and breathe Metallica. It was a lifestyle that they were accustomed to and one that would prove very difficult to change whether they wanted to or not. Metallica was family and it didn't always provide an enormous amount of time for them to arrange their personal lives and to see their loved ones and friends. They were essentially torn between Metallica and their lives as everyday human beings. Being in Metallica gave the band an extreme lifestyle but it was a lot of fun too and it was something they did not want to change even though it was, at times, difficult.

The increasingly long tours and obvious homages to other rock and metal bands would help cement Metallica's reputation as a ferocious live band; certainly one of the best in the metal scene. "Even though when we're on tour it is hard to keep in touch with the real world or whatever," explained Lars, "we don't lock ourselves in our hotel rooms for 24 hours a day, we still go out when we can and do the same shit as we've always done."[ccxiii]

The band and their entourage became a tight unit made up of roadies, techs, assistants and management. They looked after one another and enjoyed each other's company. Most of the crew had been with them for years and would drop anything and everything to tour with Metallica.

James Newsted: "We hear stories about some of these other bands. When we're not on the road, these guys go in teams – lighting team, sound team – on to other tours. And we hear stories about other bands that don't even recognise these guys. The bands work with the same guys for a year, and they don't even know their names. 'Oh you work for us? What do you do?' Things like that. It's not a relationship like Metallica has with their crew. It's a big family and therefore it makes the show happen every night in a big way… we all work hard for each other to make this thing happen. We're all proud to do our job and to make everybody else happy and proud of what they're doing. It's really good chemistry."[ccxiv]

To this day Metallica have always enjoyed paying tribute to their heroes especially British bands from the 1970s and early 1980s and the San Francisco-based thrash band, in particular Lars Ulrich, have stayed friends with the likes of Brian Tatler from Diamond Head and Lemmy from Motörhead. Metallica were essentially inspired by 'the two heads' and it's a blend of the former's fast and fierce riffs with the latter band's heavy thump and aggressive vocals that continued to give Metallica their distinctive edge.

Metallica have been more than helpful to Diamond Head and their ilk, as Brian Tatler explains: "In fact if Metallica had not covered Diamond Head the band would not have reformed in 1991 and again in 2000. I reckon Diamond Head would have faded away like so many NWOBHM bands from the1980s. And of course my share of the songwriter's royalties have come in very handy!"[ccxv]

Metallica certainly exposed a lot of the elder statesmen of metal to a younger generation. Diamond Head and many of the New Wave Of British Heavy Metal bands certainly owe a favour to Metallica for having their music exposed to a generation of metal fans that may not have been familiar with that particular era of metal. Metallica have been very gracious to their heroes and though they have taken several controversial steps in their career they have nothing but respect for their idols. They remain not just metal musicians but also metal fans, loving not only playing their own music to thousands of headbanging metal maniacs but also other bands' music too. While some bands often forget where they came from and who inspired them, Metallica have been quite the opposite.

James Hetfield: "It's just good to fuck with people, that's all… The first song of the set is always the 'Yeah, dude, all right!' song of the night, and when we come out with a cover [like Budgie's

'Breadfan'] you can tell that a lot of people don't recognise it. There's this [thing] to admit to their buddies that they don't know the song. But hopefully they'll find out from someone what the song was, and go discover the band that wrote it."[ccxvi]

Metallica recorded their first ever music video for the single 'One' in 1989. This opened up the band to a whole new audience especially as it aired on MTV. This is an interesting aspect in the early years of Metallica's career. They had initially refused to release music videos and remained something of an underground metal band with a broadening cult fanbase in the mid-1980s but with pressure from various angles they finally gave in and released the aforementioned music video. However, some fans attacked the band for going mainstream and for going against their supposed beliefs in commercial metal and reported opposition to the glossy commercialism of MTV.

Lars Ulrich said in 1988: "We came real close to doing a promo video for '(Welcome Home) Sanitarium' off ...*Puppets* and 'For Whom The Bell Tolls' off ...*Lightning*, but at the end of the day, we just sort of asked ourselves 'Why? What's the point?' But if we ever do get around to doing one, it'll have to be completely different from your typical bullshit video that you can see on MTV's 'Headbanger's Ball' because we don't wanna be associated with all the other shit that's on there."[ccxvii]

The band later released a VHS collection called *2 Of One* which featured both videos and an interview with Lars Ulrich (both videos were later included on the 2006 DVD *The Videos: 1989-2004*). They warmed to the idea of making videos and after having a good experience making 'One', they realised it was not as daunting as they initially thought.

Anyway, that song was a hit single: it peaked at Number 35 in the United States and Number 13 in the UK. They actually made two videos for the song. The first video was the band playing in an abandoned warehouse while the second video was remixed with footage from the 1971 American anti-war film *Johnny Got His Gun*, which prompted the band to buy the rights to the movie rather than license them. Initially, the remixed version of the video was submitted to MTV and just in case it was declined by the station, the band would submit the performance only version. The remix version was accepted and it has become one of the most popular metal videos in history ('One' was voted Number 38 in 'Top 100 Videos Of All Time' Poll by MTV in 1999 and has become one of MTV's most popular videos in their history).

1989 would bring some minor controversy to the band's name. They were nominated for a Grammy Award in the 'Best Hard Rock/Metal Performance Vocal Or Instrument' category. However, after the band played 'One' – the last single from *...And Justice For All* – in front of the packed auditorium in Los Angeles and though they were standing backstage, when the winner was announced they were surprised they did not hear their name rather than that of Jethro Tull (for *Crest Of A Knave*), the British progressive rock band whose lead singer Ian Anderson famously plays the flute. Tull did not attend the ceremony as they had reportedly been advised by their manager that Metallica would surely win a Grammy in such a category. This would go down in history as a major shock on behalf of the Grammy votes so much so that *Entertainment Weekly* placed it in their 'Grammy's 10 Biggest Upsets' poll.

Metallica had now gained significant mainstream exposure and were even recognised by members of the public who were not necessarily metal fans. How did they cope with the fame? Some musicians adore the notoriety both on and off stage and enjoy being recognised and worshipped by masses of people, while others retreat to their homes and go into periods of hibernation, not wanting the fame to consume every part of their lives. Kirk Hammett stated: "You can only be what the public thinks you are for so long before it becomes boring... I felt quite objectified by it all [at times]. When I met people, they'd go 'Wow, I always thought you were this big mean person. But you're really very nice – and kinda short.' A lot of people get fixated on what they need us to be – appearance-wise, how we should sound."[ccxviii]

Bigger and more commercially successful albums would follow *... And Justice For All* but none of those subsequent albums would have the impact on the metal scene as the first four releases. To this day this quartet of 'early years' records stand apart from the rest. However, there is a common opinion amongst hardcore Metallica fans that it's really only the first three albums that have the major impact and that even ...*And Justice For All*, with all its flaws, is still too weak to be considered a classic.

Where next? By this point there was a sense that Metallica wanted to move on. 'Mature' is the wrong word; perhaps 'change' is more appropriate. They did not want to be pigeonholed into one style of music. "When it comes to us defining the last twenty years of hard rock, I usually kind of shy out of that," Ulrich explained. "I guess we were blessed when we started playing, to have something that was kind of unique and different. A big part of it is the fact that we always had a bunch of people that we never had personality issues with."[ccxix]

They had ideas in mind for something different. "We're more than just metal, okay," confessed James Newsted a decade later. "That's the thing. [Fans] want us to be just in this little thing right here, and we're not happy with that. I love playing 'Battery', 'Whiplash', 'Damage'. Those are my favourites too, don't get me wrong now 'cause we're in the same boat with that, but you have to realise and respect us for being musicians and wanting to grow."[ccxx]

The band had progressed enormously not only as a collective unit but also individual musicians. "Remember, at that time, when *Kill 'Em All* and *Ride The Lightning* came out, heavy metal was not that popular at all," said Hammett years later. "There were all these other different types of music that were more popular at the time. Back then heavy metal bands stood out like sore thumbs and people didn't really understand heavy metal. We just thought we'd record a few albums and go out on tour but we definitely didn't expect it to be like this."[ccxxi]

They'd all come a long way since the days of *Kill 'Em All* and with the rigours of touring life and the constant rehearsals they'd tightened their playing skills, refined and polished their talents. James Newsted on Hetfield: "As an instrumentalist in heavy music he's the best, and to be able to play with him is an honour.

That's all there is to it. I've always felt that way about it and I will always feel that way about it. He taught me a lot of shit and help me develop my playing style and become who I am as a musician. I have great respect in that way."[ccxxii]

Former *Kerrang!* journalist Xavier Russell believes, "I think they are still the best three albums. The production was very varied on the first three albums. *Kill 'Em All*, was naturally a bit rough round the edges, due to budget and the recording studio and the band were still very much in their infancy and learning their craft. *Ride The Lightning* is still my favourite Metallica album, mainly because of the production and the songs. You listen to it today and it still sounds fresh. I was in The Crobar [famous central London rock pub] recently and 'For Whom The Bell Tolls' came blasting out, and it still sends a shiver down my spine all these years later. *Master Of Puppets* meanwhile is a good album but is sadly over-produced and therefore lacks the intensity it should have. Don't get me started on ...*And Justice For All.* When I first heard that I screamed, 'Where's the bass!'"[ccxxiii]

John Ricci of the Canadian speed metal band Exciter said to the author: "I really like all of Metallica's albums including the first four albums, but I would say during that time we were making new exciting music as well without noticing what Metallica were doing. I would say Metallica (respectfully speaking) were not an influence at all on us. When we finally discovered our own style we only knew of Metallica through cassette demo tapes and whatever buzz we heard in the music industry. I think their first four albums [made an] impact on the whole world because it was so intense and fast and the general metal listener was accustomed to listening to older school bands from the 1970s, so the speed and intensity in Metallica's music took everyone by surprise."[ccxxiv]

Bob Nalbandian, who was an integral figure in the East Coast metal writing scene along with Rob Quintana et al, says that Metallica's first four albums are so important not only in the band's back-catalogue but also in the entire history of metal "because they are arguably their best efforts and totally groundbreaking metal albums! I think they were so young and hungry and full of testosterone at that time and they just captured every bit of that energy on those first four records. Not to mention the songs are amazing!"[ccxxv]

The 1980s were over and Metallica had not only made a significant imprint in metal culture but also popular culture as a whole. "I think that Metallica has so much more to offer than just playing fast," explained Newsted in 1992. "Metallica definitely started a new thing in the 1980s. We definitely had something to do with influencing a number of bands to do what they're doing now and that is a compliment to us... We've just done our thing. It worked and it made some people happy. Any band that has any kind of substance is going to grow and take chances, with different musics [*sic*] and instruments and go outside their realm a little bit. And that's kind of what Metallica has always done, just grown each time they make a record and each time they do a tour."[ccxxvi]

When asked if he thought Metallica would become such a successful band, Brian Slagel of Metal Blade Records says, "None of us did, never in a million years. We were all just metal fans trying to do things for the scene. When we get together now, sometimes it is, 'How did this all happen?' It really is amazing to see how big they have become."[ccxxvii]

On the same subject, photographer Bill Hale comments, "Metallica had 'it'! Whatever 'it' was, but they had it! Metallica was just the band for and of its time. They started out as four 'friends' in a band, had a few line-up changes, toured their asses off but they never forgot their fans or where they came from and that is why they are still going strong after all these years!"[ccxxviii]

Bob Nalbandian says, "Never in a million years. I thought they had the potential to be big on an underground level like a Motörhead or something, but never did I think they would become the biggest metal band in the world!"[ccxxix]

In the following decade Metallica became a different sort of a band; they left their thrash metal roots behind and followed a more mainstream, commercial avenue of metal. Nevertheless, their roots are firmly planted in thrash metal and their earlier releases remain benchmarks of the genre and that is why the early years of Metallica's history are so significant within the realms of metal.

Exciter's John Ricci says, "I think their early albums set a standard that every aspiring metal band was forced to follow; every new band was measured by Metallica's success which definitely put pressure [on] to these young bands. I think that's why a lot of bands sound like Metallica or have heavily borrowed ideas from Metallica."[ccxxx]

Lars Ulrich: "I really feel comfortable with this age thing in rock and roll. I don't feel like just because I'm in Metallica, it has to be a totally youthful thing. This unwritten rule in rock where you have to get out when you get old – fuck that. We can keep doing what we're doing without letting age get in the way."[ccxxxi]

Afterword
by John Tucker

Author of *Suzie Smiled…The New Wave Of British Heavy Metal* and collaborator with Brian Tatler on his autobiography, *Am I Evil?*

Metallica, the NWOBHM and Diamond Head…

It's the stuff of dreams, really. Inspired by the New Wave Of British Heavy Metal and almost obsessed by a track called 'It's Electric', a young man hops on a plane and flies halfway round the world to see his favourite band. He even gets to meet them after the show. In the ensuing conversation he reveals that he hasn't put any thought into what happens next: he's come straight from the airport to the gig and has no idea where he's going to stay. The guitarist, mightily impressed with the guy's determination, suggests he comes and stays with the band, and he does, spending the first few nights at the guitarist's house and then later staying with the singer – and their respective parents! All the while the kid not only snaps up all the NWOBHM releases he can get his hands on, but also watches his favourite band as they write, rehearse and perform songs, soaking everything up. When he returns to the States he places a 'Musicians Wanted' ad, and Metallica is born.

The enormity of the meeting between the young Lars Ulrich and Diamond Head in July, 1981 cannot be understated, and can probably best be measured by the 'What if's.' What if Ulrich had missed the gig? What if the members of the band hadn't wanted to engage with their fans that night? What if the young soon-to-be drummer hadn't been given the opportunity to hang out with the band, had not learned how to craft a song or what it takes to keep a band on the road. Quite simply, there would not have been a Metallica; or had Ulrich eventually formed such a band anyway it would not have been as inspirational and pivotal to the development of metal as it is today.

The sound of the band's early albums, which went on to influence so many other acts, was highly influenced by the NWOBHM in general and Diamond Head in particular. In Metallica, Ulrich took the style of the NWOBHM (and the aggression of Motörhead) and infused it with both his and Hetfield's own enthusiasm and the burgeoning local sound to develop a hybrid which soon became the springboard for the speed/thrash metal boom of the mid-1980s.

Metallica's early sets featured a number of NWOBHM covers including the likes of Blitzkrieg's 'Blitzkrieg', Savage's 'Let It Loose' and Sweet Savage's 'Killing Time' as well as 'Helpless', 'Sucking My Love', 'Am I Evil?' and 'The Prince' – quite a healthy chunk of Diamond Head's first LP. And as they began to write their own material, the nods to Sean Harris's and Brian Tatler's songs and style were as obvious as the beers in the Americans' hands. From the speed of their tunes, to the numerous riffs and time-changes in lengthy sprawling compositions, the bulk of the material on *Kill 'Em All* drew heavily on Ulrich's fascination with Diamond Head. Let's not forget that not only were Diamond Head one of the fastest bands around at that time, but they'd also been awarded the accolade of having 'more great riffs in a single song than Sabbath had on their first four albums,' and there's no way either fact escaped the young drummer. 'Hit The Lights' and 'The Prince' are more than just distant cousins – the pacing, the construction, the frenetic lead breaks; and the section just before Hammett's solo is pure Harris/Tatler. The time change midway through 'The Four Horsemen', the middle section of 'Whiplash' (ironically, in this case the slower part of the song), the opening and ending to 'No

Remorse' (which also features some trademark Iron Maiden runs) – it's all there [as an influence] in the material that was being composed in a bedroom in Stourbridge several years earlier. In fact, pretty much the only part of the album that doesn't have some kind of relationship with Diamond Head is Cliff Burton's bass solo.

By *Ride The Lightning* Metallica were beginning to develop their own style [more], although the comparisons are still apparent in some of the riffs, the length of the songs and the fact that neither band was really comfortable with trying to write commercial songs to order: 'Escape', Metallica's one real attempt at writing a 'single' – not that it was ever released as such – sounds as unconvincing and unhappy as Diamond Head's 'Call Me'.

"Diamond Head were 50% of what ended up being Metallica," Ulrich once famously admitted and to Metallica's credit they've never attempted to disguise the fact; in fact, they have gone out of the way to help all the bands that influenced them by recording covers of their songs and thus earning royalties for them. Metallica's biggest debt though is definitely owed to Diamond Head, and this was finally repaid in July, 2011 when the massed ranks of the Big Four of thrash metal flanked Tatler at Sonisphere for a massive rendition of 'Am I Evil?'. The smile on the English guitarist's face said it all.

John Tucker
www.johntuckeronline.com
September, 2011

Part II

The Aftermath

APPENDIX I

METALLICA – THOSE THAT CAME AFTER...

(1990-2011)

"You think one day some fucker's gonna tell you, 'You have a Number 1 record in America,' and the whole world will ejaculate... I stood there in my hotel room, and there was this fax that said, 'You're Number 1'. And it was, like, 'Well, okay.' It was just another fucking fax from the office."

Lars Ulrich[ccxxxii]

Grunge music had a lot to do with the shape, sound and ultimately, the downfall of hard rock and heavy metal in the 1990s. That said, bands like Metallica and Guns N' Roses had survived the movement remarkably well (which was somewhat reminiscent of the way Queen had endured the punk era back in the mid-to-late 1970s) whereas a lot of lesser-known rock and metal bands lost record deals and saw their ticket sales drop alarmingly. Hard rock and heavy metal didn't completely disappear; it just went underground and dropped out of the public's consciousness until a time came when it would become fashionable again.

Grunge was like punk in that it was anti-establishment and anti-authoritarian and whereas punk was an obvious reaction to prog rock, grunge was a reaction to pampered poodle-haired LA metal. Seattle shaped the sound of American music in the late 1980s and early 1990s and non-grunge bands that were still in the same depressive, alternative rock-vibe like REM were also becoming extremely popular. Grunge fans – christened 'loser kids' by some – wore flannel shirts and ripped jeans; they looked like the kind of youths that alternative dorky-lookin' students would buy drugs from at college campuses whilst chatting about Nietzsche's philosophy and Nicolas Roeg films. At least that's the impression they gave.

The biggest bands of the grunge scene included most obviously Nirvana, Pearl Jam (who were big fans of English hard rockers UFO), Soundgarden and Alice In Chains. The latter two bands were certainly heavy enough to appeal to metal fans and even some of their influences were metal, notably the Godfathers of the genre, Black Sabbath. However, grunge, just like all music movements, came to an abrupt end. Nirvana's tormented frontman Kurt Cobain killed himself in April, 1994.

While all this turbulent history was being shaped, Metallica were enclosed in a self-contained bubble with all the various musical trends passing them by while they did their own thing and their hardened fanbase followed their every move. Though this book is specifically about the early years of Metallica during their ascent to the top of metal's premiere league, it is worth giving an overview of their albums post *...And Justice For All.* This chronology of their albums from the 1990s onwards will help place those first four albums into some kind of context within the band's entire history. Certainly *after* the release of *...And Justice For All* they achieved more success with their fifth album than even they could have predicted...

In October, 1990, Metallica recorded their fifth album at the One On One Studio in Hollywood with the revered and appropriately named Bob Rock, known for his work with Aerosmith, Bon Jovi, The Cult and famously Mötley Crüe on their hair metal classic *Dr. Feelgood.* They had a batch of songs which had been written over a two-month period during the summer and had recorded demos in mid-September. Metallica and Rock spent about a week recording at Little Mountain Sound Studios in Vancouver, the home of the influential and highly respected producer Bruce Fairbairn (RIP) and Rock himself. It wasn't an easy album to make by any standards and the costs of the sessions were huge (after three remixes, figures of $1 million dollars were reported in some magazines). The album also brought some personal upheavals. There were clashes of personalities and creative differences between the band and Rock, especially in the early weeks, which have been publically acknowledged by both parties. However, the partnership soon produced dividends. Rock had changed the way the band had previously recorded: for example, he would have them record their parts together rather than separately. After the release of the fifth album, hardcore Metallica zealots even went so far as to create a petition to stop Rock from producing any more Metallica albums.

When *Metallica* (dubbed *The Black Album* by fans due to its black cover sleeve) was released in August, 1991, it hit Number 1 in ten countries, including their native United States. It gave the band their first dose of major global mainstream attention. It spawned six singles: 'Enter Sandman', 'Don't Tread On Me', 'The Unforgiven', 'Nothing Else Matters', 'Wherever I May Roam' and 'Sad But True'. Since its release it has sold 22 million copies worldwide making it one of the most successful albums in history, regardless of genre boundaries. The album has since been featured in many polls, including *Rolling Stone*'s 'Essential Recordings Of The 90s', *Spin* magazine's '90 Greatest Albums Of The 90s' and Q magazine's 'Best Metal Albums Of All Time'.

Metal writer and Metallica fan Bob Nalbandian says, "I actually really loved *The Black Album*, and still do. I think they pretty much did all they could as far as making a thrash album after *Justice* and rather than repeating themselves they recorded a totally different, but equally classic recording with *The Black Album*."[ccxxxiii]

Is it true to say the earlier, thrash metal sound of the band died when bassist Cliff Burton did? "Not quite," says Metallica and Cliff Burton biographer Joel McIver. "The biggest leap came between *Justice* and *The Black Album*, three years after his death."[ccxxxiv]

When asked if it was obvious Metallica would become such a popular band globally, former *Kerrang!* journalist and Metallica fan Xavier Russell says, "Yes, I did think the band would become massively popular. And while I liked *The Black Album* it wasn't a patch on their first three studio albums. I remember when I first saw the band in 1981, saying to [journalists] Geoff Barton, Malcolm Dome and Dante Bonutto that Metallica will become the biggest band on the planet by 1991. I was proved right when *The Black Album* came out; in 1991 Metallica had become a monster."[ccxxxv]

In November, 1993, Metallica released their first ever live album *Live Shit: Binge & Purge.* The original release contained three CDs and three video tapes with concerts recorded in Mexico City on the Nowhere Else To Roam Tour while the more recent collection houses two DVDs with concerts recorded in San Diego and Seattle. It peaked at Number 26 in the United States. Live albums are rarely big success stories.

The controversial (amongst fans, anyway) sixth album *Load*, was recorded at The Plant Studio in Sausalito, California over the course of several months between May, 1995 and February, 1996. The band had around thirty demos to work with. Again with producer Bob Rock, the sound of the album was markedly different from *Metallica* and especially their first four albums. *Load* was far removed from the traditional American thrash sound with heavy blues influences and a mainstream heavy metal sound. It remains their longest studio record. Released in June, 1996, almost a full five years since *Metallica,* the album hit Number 1 in the United States and sold over half-a-million copies in its first week of release in the US alone and has since gone on to sell a staggering five million worldwide. However, despite *Load* being received with only luke-warm reviews by fans, many critics appreciated the band's shift in sound.

ReLoad was a sort of sequel or companion to 1996's *Load.* The initial idea was to release a double album but that proved too difficult in terms of recording so many songs at once so the band later recorded some more tracks between June 1997 and October at The Plant Studio in Sausalito. Perhaps due to the (relative) lack of public enthusiasm surrounding *Load*, *ReLoad* sold less than half-a-million copies in the United States during its first week of release and has sold about a million less worldwide than *Load.*

Nonetheless, the album peaked at Number 1 in the United

States and Number 4 in the UK. Four singles were released from the album: 'The Memory Remains', 'The Unforgiven II', 'Fuel' and 'Better Than You'. The latter single won the band a Grammy Award for 'Best Metal Performance'.

In November, 1998, Metallica released the double CD covers collection called *Garage Inc.* which contained the whole of the previously out of print *The $5.98 EP: Garage Days Revisited* as well as new covers that had been recorded at The Plant Studios between September and October of 1998. Many of the songs featured were NWOBHM bands that had inspired Metallica in the first place. The success of the album (over two million copies sold worldwide) meant that the artists covered would receive not only a higher degree of recognition but also royalties. The artists covered include Diamond Head, Holocaust, Killing Joke, Budgie, Misfits, Blitzkrieg, Queen, Anti-Nowhere League, Sweet Savage and Motörhead. Reviews of the double album were strong.

The album peaked at Number 2 in the United States and the following singles were released: 'Turn The Page', 'Die, Die My Darling' and 'Whiskey In The Jar'. The latter won the band a Grammy Award for 'Best Metal Performance'.

On April 21 and 22, 1999, Metallica played and recorded both shows with the San Francisco Symphony Orchestra (conducted by the revered Michael Kamen) at the Berkeley Community Theatre. Metallica drew inspiration from the 1969 Deep Purple opus *Concerto For Group And Orchestra* although the original idea for a heavy metal band to play live with an orchestra was perhaps inspired by the late bassist Cliff Burton who had a deep fondness for classical works. Released in November 1999, *S&M*, as it was dubbed, reached Number 2 in the United States and Number 1 in Australia. It sold around 300,000 copies in its first week of release. Reviews were mostly positive.

It was the last album to feature bassist James Newsted who left the band on January 17, 2001. He was later replaced by Robert Trujillo, formerly of Suicidal Tendencies and Ozzy Osbourne's own band.

In June, 2003, Metallica released possibly the most reviled album in their career thus far. *St. Anger* was produced by Bob

Rock from May 2002 to April 2003. In January 2001, the band had rented an army barracks in the Presidio area of San Francisco and turned it into a makeshift studio. The album was delayed due to the aforementioned departure of Newsted and James Hetfield's stint in rehab for 'alcoholism and other addictions'. The band were undergoing massive internal struggles so much so they hired a personal enhancement coach by the name of Phil Towle. The making of the album was caught on film by Joe Berlinger and Bruce Sinofsky and released as the critically acclaimed award-winning rock documentary *Some Kind Of Monster*. It took two years to make and used over one thousand hours of film. During the recording of the album Ulrich turned off the snare sound on his drum which created an entirely different effect far removed from his rock and thrash metal roots; this received a massive backlash from fans who did not take to the new drum sound at all (among many other aspects that were disliked). *St. Anger* sold just over 400,000 copies in its first week of release and hit Number 1 in their native country and Number 3 in the UK. It also hit Number in Australia, Austria, Canada, Finland, Germany, Japan, Norway, Poland and Sweden. Reviews were decidedly mixed.

"I think with *Load*, *Reload* and *St. Anger* they may have lost their focus too much!" says the expert metal writer Bob Nalbandian.[ccxxxvi] Nonetheless, the title-track won the band a Grammy Award for 'Best Metal Performance.' Just four singles were released from the album: 'St. Anger', 'Frantic', 'The Unnamed Feeling' and 'Some Kind Of Monster'.

Between May, 2007 and April of the following year, Metallica worked on their ninth studio album with producer Rick Rubin. The band had opted out of working with Bob Rock (whom they'd collaborated with on every album since 1991's *Metallica*). It was a bold attempt to go back to their thrash metal roots with long and technically accomplished solos and thrash metal riffs (whereas *St. Anger* contained no solos, minimal production and a modern sound). The album was recorded at three studios on the West Coast: Sound City Studios in Van Nuys, California, Shangri La Studios in Malibu, California, and HQ in San Rafael,

California. The resulting record – *Death Magnetic* – was also their first album to be released via Universal. It was released in September, 2008 and hit Number 1 in the United States, making it their fifth album to do so. In just its first three days of release, *Death Magnetic* sold almost half-a-million copies and peaked at Number 1 in an incredible 34 countries, including the UK. It received four Grammy Award nominations and was in many end of year polls, including ones printed by *Q*, *Uncut*, *TIME*, *Revolver*, *Rolling Stone*, *Metal Edge*, *Metal Hammer*, *Metal Maniacs* and *Kerrang!*. By mid-2010, *Death Magnetic* had sold 4.5 million copies worldwide.

Death Magnetic was a major triumph for the band and while it may not be as groundbreaking or masterful as those albums from the 1980s, it was nevertheless a significant step in the right direction after the abysmal *St. Anger.*

In October, 2011, Metallica released a collaborative album with Lou Reed, formally of the legendary New York band, The Velvet Underground. The album was rather bizarrely named *Lulu*. The roots of the collaboration went back to the 2009 Rock And Roll Hall Of Fame's 25th Anniversary Concert where they both performed. They began working together two years later. Recording had been completed in June, 2011 and released at the tail-end of October. One of America's top rock writers, David Fricke of *Rolling Stone,* had been privileged enough to hear a couple of tracks from the album prior to its release and compared it to a combination of Reed's 1973 *Berlin* and Metallica's 1986 *Master Of Puppets*.

However, what was on the surface an intriguing collaboration did not meet with positive reviews – to say the least. Writing in the rock magazine *Fireworks*, the author's own thoughts reflected those of the majority of fellow rock writers. "Not in recent memory has an album caused such a god-almighty backlash as *Lulu*. While Metallica's peers Anthrax and Megadeth have recently released excellent albums with *Worship Music* and *Th1rt3en*, respectively, Metallica have released not only their weakest album to date but one of the poorest metal albums in recent memory; possibly in the history of metal."

Metallica have yet to make anything as groundbreaking as those first four albums; as mentioned already, many fans would go further and highlight only the first three records. Those albums represent a period in their career when they were young, hungry and just *different*. They were angry too. Very angry. Since then, they have never been afraid to move on and change and adapt their sound and musical identity. Perhaps it's the case that they'll never make anything as bold or technically accomplished as *Master Of Puppets* and whether that's because Cliff Burton was in the band will never been known, only speculated. *Kill 'Em All*, *Ride The Lightning* and *Master Of Puppets* proved that Burton was a fundamental figure in Metallica; it can be argued that he was certainly the most technical. Regardless of the mixed responses, *...And Justice For All* was certainly a strong album despite the obvious change in musical direction from its three predecessors. It marked the end of an era for sure and the records that came after were nowhere near as profound.

Will Metallica ever end? Will they call it a day?

"Well, death doesn't stop it, pyrotechnics don't stop it, people leaving don't stop it," Hetfield said to writer Greg Pratt. "Yeah, what does stop it? Bus accidents, all that, I don't know. I think when Lars and I decide to not do it or we don't feel it or something happens to one of us then it probably stops. But that doesn't mean the spirit of Metallica or the love for it stops."[ccxxxvii]

APPENDIX II

AMERICAN THRASH METAL – A RETROSPECTIVE TRIBUTE

"Peers are anybody you respect and admire, if I understand the word correctly."

Lars Ulrich[ccxxxviii]

Metallica was certainly not the only American thrash metal band of the 1980s; there were many others but none of them were as wildly successful or popular as Metallica. Here is a *selected* list (complete with a potted history) of some of the most influential and successful thrash metal bands of that era.

Metal photographer Bill Hale who shot the rise of Metallica and Megadeth in the early days, sums the subject up rather well: "Way before Metallica and Megadeth came along, the Bay Area had some great bands already: Vicious Rumors, Exodus, Trauma, Griffin, Anvil Chorus, Death Angel, Testament, Lääz Rockit, Heathen, Forbidden, Blind Illusion, Ruffians, Vio-lence, Possessed, just to name a few... But somehow Metallica rose to the top of the 'Thrash Metal Heap.' The Bay Area has always been a hot bed for music. The 1980s was just the heavy metal chapter!"[ccxxxix]

NOTE: This list is restricted exclusively to American bands that formed or were active throughout the 1980s and therefore discounts Canadian thrash/speed metal bands such as Annihilator, Anvil, Exciter and Voivod and European thrashers Destruction, Kreator and Sodom and Brazil's Sepultura et al.

LEAGUE 1

ANTHRAX

Formed in New York City in 1981, Anthrax was founded by guitarists Scott Ian and Danny Lilker. They would become part of the Big Four of thrash metal making them one of the genre's fundamental bands. The band has had a number of line-up changes and several internal complications, notably going through four singers: Neil Turbin, Joey Belladonna, Dan Nelson and John Bush. The classic line-up is seen by many as from the *Among The Living* era with singer Joey Belladonna, guitarists Dan Spitz and Scott Ian, bassist Frank Bello and drummer Charlie Benante. They continue to tour regularly though their studio output has slowed down in recent years.

Key albums: *Spreading The Disease* (1985), *Among The Living* (1987), *State Of Euphoria* (1988) and *Persistence Of Time* (1990).

Anthrax

MEGADETH

Megadeth was of course formed by Dave Mustaine after he was ousted from Metallica in 1983. Mustaine was joined by bassist Dave Ellefson and Greg Handevidt. They would become one of the genre's most successful bands and would join Metallica and Anthrax as part of the Big Four. After the release of their debut album *Killing Is My Business… And Business Is Good*, Lars Ulrich told *Metal Forces'* Bernard Doe: "I was expecting the first album to be a lot like Metallica, but I think it's great Dave's taken a completely different approach and tried to be totally different to anything we had done with him."[ccxl]

What Mustaine had done was form a band and turned it into a living breathing animal that was totally separate from Metallica. Megadeth have their own sound and identity that is different from Mustaine's former band. There have been many line-up changes in Megadeth's long history and in 2002, the band was briefly on ice after Mustaine had nerve damage on his left arm. With thirty million albums sold worldwide and ten Top 40 albums in the United States, their legacy is assured. They released their thirteenth album, *TH1RT3EN*, in 2011.

Key albums: *Killing Is My Business… And Business Is Good* (1985), *Peace Sells… But Who's Buying?* (1986), *So Far, So Good… So What!* (1988) and *Rust In Peace* (1990).

Megadeth
© photo courtesy of Red Shaw

SLAYER

From Huntington Park in California, Slayer was formed in 1981 by guitarists Kerry King and Jeff Hanneman. Slayer was the final part of the Big Four of thrash metal with Metallica, Megadeth and Anthrax. Lars Ulrich told *Metal Forces'* Bernard Doe back in 1984: "About a year and a half ago in LA, we were headlining and Slayer were at the bottom of a four-band bill. They played all cover versions, like Priest, Purple and Maiden."[ccxli]

Slayer did indeed start as a covers band with glam influences before they started playing what is now referred to as thrash metal. There's no doubt some of the NWOBHM bands had an influence on them.

With singer Tom Araya and drummer Dave Lombardo completing the classic line-up, Slayer released eleven studio albums between their 1983 debut *Show No Mercy* and 2009's *World Painted Blood*.

Key albums: *Hell Awaits* (1985), *Reign In Blood* (1986), *South Of Heaven* (1988) and *Seasons In The Abyss* (1990).

Slayer
© photo courtesy of Red Shaw

LEAGUE II

EXODUS

Formed in Richmond, California in 1980, Exodus may never have received the high reverence and commercial success of Metallica and their ilk but they remain one of the genre's key bands. The very first line-up of Exodus consisted of guitarists Kirk Hammett and Tim Agnello, drummer Tom Hunting, bassist Carlton Melson and singer Keith Stewart. Their debut *Bonded By Blood* was released in 1984. The band has undergone several line-up changes and there was in a period in the 1990s when they remained inactive but then resumed work in 2001. Between 1984 and 2010 they released ten studio albums; they continue to tour regularly.

Key albums: *Pleasures Of The Flesh* (1987), *Fabulous Disaster* (1988) and *Impact Is Imminent* (1990).

SUICIDAL TENDENCIES

Formed in 1981 in Venice, LA, Suicidal Tendencies is a thrash-hardcore punk crossover band whose long-lasting founder and only permanent member Mike Muir is one of the genre's leading frontmen. They're hardly prolific with only eight studio albums released between their 1983 self-titled debut and 2000's *Free Your Soul And Save Your Mind* although they have briefly disbanded a couple of times, notably between 1995 and 1997. Despite their hardcore punk inspired beginnings, they have been embraced by thrash metal fans.

Key albums: *Suicidal Tendencies* (1983), *Join The Army* (1987) and *How Will I Laugh Tomorrow When I Can't Even Smile Today?* (1988).

TESTAMENT

A pivotal thrash metal band, Testament formed in Berkeley, California in 1983 and released their debut *The Legacy* in 1987.

Testament's profile rose when they supported Anthrax around the United States and Europe in support of Anthrax's *Among The Living* album, which is regarded a thrash metal classic. The band has gone through several line-up amendments leaving the original members Eric Peterson, guitarist Alex Skolnick and bassist Greg Christian to lead the group. They toured Europe in 2009 with Judas Priest and Megadeth as part of the *Priest Feast* Tour. Between their 1987 debut and 2008's *The Formation Of Damnation* they released nine studio albums in total. They are a revered thrash metal band though outside of the genre they have gained less prominence but continue to have a cult following globally.

Key albums: *The New Order* (1988), *Practice What You Preach* (1989), *Souls Of Black* (1990) and *The Ritual* (1992).

LEAGUE III

ATTITUDE ADJUSTMENT

Formed in 1985 in the Bay Area of San Francisco, Attitude Adjustment are one of the notable thrash bands from the northern California metal scene. They released their thrash-hardcore crossover album *American Paranoia* in 1985. Their second and final album *Out Of Hand* was released in 1991. The band's founder Chris Kontos went on to form the very successful metal band Machine Head with Robb Flynn of the thrash band Vio-Lence.

Key albums: *American Paranoia* (1985) and *Out Of Hand* (1991).

BLIND ILLUSION

Blind Illusion were heavily influenced by prog rock bands Rush and Jethro Tull hence their progressive thrash sound. The band was formed in 1979 while guitarist and songwriter Marc

Biedermann was still at high school. The band went through many line-up changes throughout its history with Biedermann as its only constant member. Their debut album *The Sane Asylum* was released in 1988 but they wouldn't release their second album until 2010's *Demon Master.* The band broke up in 1989 and then reformed in 2009 hence the length between releases.

Key albums: *The Sane Asylum* (1988) and *Demon Master* (2010).

DEATH ANGEL

Death Angel formed in Concord, California in 1982 but the first phase of their career would only last until 1991, before resuming work in 2001. Prior to releasing their first major label album on Geffen in 1990 with *Act III*, they had independently released two albums: 1987's *The Ultra-Violence* and 1988's *Frolic Through The Park.* There have been many amendments to the band's line-up throughout their history with singer Mark Osegueda and guitarist Rob Cavestany being constant members.

Key albums: *Frolic Through The Park* (1988), *Act III* (1990) and *The Art Of Dying* (2004).

DEFIANCE

Formed in Oakland, California in 1985, Defiance is a relatively obscure thrash metal band known by enthusiasts for their technical brilliance and exhilarating live shows. The first phase of the band's career lasted until 1994. After a couple of demos their debut album, *Product Of Society,* was released in 1989 with their most recent album being 2009's *The Prophecy*.

Key albums: *Product Of Society* (1989), *Void Terra Firma* (1990) and *Beyond Recognition* (1992).

EPIDEMIC

This Bay Area thrash band formed in 1985 and also crossed over into the death metal genre, but later disbanded in 1995. The band's name is derived from a Slayer song and they released their debut *The Truth Of What Will Be* in 1990. Two more albums followed but the band folded after their third release after some internal differences and record company issues. They were not a prolific band but made an excellent reputation as a furious live act, particularly on the 1993 tour with Cannibal Corpse and Unleashed.

Key albums: *The Truth Of What Will Be* (1990), *Decameron* (1992) and *Exit Paradise* (1994).

FORBIDDEN

This Bay Area thrash band was initially formed in 1985 by drummer Jim Pittman and guitarist Robb Flynn under the moniker Forbidden Evil before they shortened their monicker. Their debut *Forbidden Evil* was released in 1988. They have broken up a couple of times but are still active in the 2010s. They remain one of the most influential Bay Area thrash bands of all time. However, they have struggled on a commercial level to gain higher prominence outside of the genre. Nevertheless, they are an important band in the beginnings of the Bay Area thrash scene in Northern California.

Key albums: *Forbidden Evil* (1988), *Twisted Into Form* (1990) and *Green* (1997).

HEATHEN

Formed in the Bay Area in 1984 by guitarist Lee Atlus and drummer Carl Sacco, Heathen released the *Pray For Death* demo in 1986 and two full-length albums before they broke up in 1993 only to reform in 2002 and release the *Recovered* EP a year later and then *The Evolution Of Chaos* in 2010. Like Metallica, Heathen have a strong NWOBHM influence in their sound, certainly on their earlier work before they began to develop their own musical identity.

Key albums: *Breaking The Silence* (1987), *Victims Of Deception* (1991) and *The Evolution Of Chaos* (2010).

LÄÄZ ROCKIT

Lääz Rockit began life as a power metal band before they began to introduce thrash metal riffs into their music. Though they remain a relatively obscure name in mainstream commercial terms, each album is highly thought of by aficionados and critics of the genre. Their debut *City's Gonna Burn* was released in 1984 but they later broke up in 1992. Some former members created the groove metal outfit Gack. They reformed in 2005 and released *Left For Dead* in 2008.

Key albums: *City's Gonna Burn* (1984), *No Stranger To Danger* (1985) and *Know Your Enemy* (1987).

SADUS

Founded in Antioch, California in 1984, Sadus were initially heavily influenced by Slayer and as such there is a lot of heavy riffing and gruff vocals on much of their earlier work, before they harnessed their own unique sound. The band line-up has been fairly consistent with singer/guitarist Darren Travis, singer/bassist Steve DiGiorgio and drummer John Allen with ex-guitarist Rob Moore. They released the *D.T.P.* demo in 1986 with their latest album released in 2006, *Out For Blood*.

Key albums: *Illusions* (1988) and *Swallowed In Black* (1990).

S.O.D.

Stormtroopers Of Death was formed in 1985 by Anthrax guitarist Scott Ian after he finished laying down his guitars for the Anthrax opus *Spreading The Disease*. He roped in the talents of fellow Anthrax buddy Charlie Benante on drums, former Anthrax bassist Dan Lilker and singer Billy Milano (Psychos frontman). It's been an on-and-off project since its inception. They released their debut album *Speak English Or Die* in 1985 and followed it up with the live album *Live At Budokan* three years later. *Bigger Than the Devil* was issued in 1999 and their most recent release was a collection of older, previously unreleased material called *Rise Of The Infidels* (2007).

Key albums: *Speak English Or Die* (1985) and *Bigger Than The Devil* (2007).

VIO-LENCE

Formed in the Bay Area in 1985, Vio-Lence was initiated by Forbidden guitarist Robb Flynn who later found fame in Machine Head. Perhaps the best known line-up of the band was singer Sean Killian, guitarists Robb Flynn and Phil Demmel, bassist Deen Dell and drummer Perry Strickland. Flynn left in 1992. Their debut album *Eternal Nightmare* was released in 1988 and they followed it up with two more full length studio albums. They reunited briefly in 2002 without Flynn. Also, Demmel joined Machine Head in 2003.

Key albums: *Eternal Nightmare* (1988), *Oppressing The Masses* (1990) and *Nothing To Gain* (1993).

APPENDIX III
SELECTED DISCOGRAPHY
(1981-1989)

ALBUMS

Kill 'Em All: *Hit The Lights/The Four Horsemen/Motorbreath/Jump In The Fire/(Anesthesia) Pulling Teeth/Whiplash/Phantom Lord/No Remorse/Seek & Destroy/Metal Militia*
CD – Megaforce 1983
(NOTE: Reissued in 1988 by Elektra with bonus tracks 'Am I Evil?' and 'Blitzkrieg')

Ride The Lightning: *Fight Fire With Fire/Ride The Lightning/For Whom The Bell Tolls/Fade To Black/Trapped Under Ice/Escape/Creeping Death/The Call Of Ktulu (Instrumental)*
CD – Megaforce 1984

Master Of Puppets: *Battery/Master Of Puppets/The Thing That Should Not Be/Welcome Home (Sanitarium)/Disposable Heroes/Leper Messiah/Orion (Instrumental)/Damage, Inc.*
CD – Elektra 1986

...And Justice For All: *Blackened/...And Justice For All/Eye Of The Beyolder/One/The Shortest Sorrow/Harvester Of Sorrow/The Frayed Ends Of Sanity/To Live Is To Die/Dyers Eve*
CD – Elektra 1988

EPs

The $5.98 EP: Garage Days Revisited: *Helpless/The Small Hours/The Wait/Crash Course In Brain Surgery/Last Caress/Green Hell*
CD – Elektra 1987

SINGLES

Whiplash *(1983)*
Jump In The Fire *(1983)*
Seek & Destroy *(1983)*
Fade To Black *(1984)*
Creeping Death *(1984)*
For Whom The Bell Tolls *(1985)*
Master Of Puppets *(1986)*
Battery *(1986)*
Welcome Home (Sanitarium) *(1986)*
Harvester Of Sorrow *(1988)*
Eye Of The Beholder *(1988)*
...And Justice For All *(1988)*
One *(1989)*

DEMOS

Ron McGovney's '82 Garage Demo *(1982)*
Power Metal *(1982)*
No Life 'Til Leather *(1982)*
Metal Up Your Ass *(Live) (1982)*
Horsemen Of The Apocalypse *(1982)*
Megaforce *(1983)*
Ride The Lightning Demos *(1983)*
Master Of Puppets Demos *(1985)*
...And Justice For All Demos *(1988)*

OTHER APPEARANCES

Metal Massacre, Vol 1 *(Track: Hit The Lights)*
CD – Metal Blade 1982

VHS/DVD

Cliff 'Em All
VHS & DVD – Elektra 1987

2 Of One
VHS – Elektra 1989

MUSIC VIDEOS

One *(1989)*
Directors: Bill Pope, Michael Saloman

TOURS

***Kill 'Em All* For One Tour** *(Headliners)*
March 5, 1984 – September 3, 1984; North America.

Seven Dates Of Hell Tour *(Support to Venom)*
February 3, 1984 – August 29, 1984; Europe.

Bang That Head That Doesn't Bang Tour *(Headliners)*
November 16, 1984 – December 20, 1984; Europe.

Ride The Lightning Tour *(Headliners)*
January 9, 1985 – December 31, 1985; North America, Europe.

Damage, Inc. Tour *(Headliners)*
March 27, 1986 – February 13, 1987; World.

Damaged Justice Tour *(Headliners)*
September 11, 1988 – October 8, 1989; World.

APPENDIX IV
SELECTED TIMELINE
(1981-1989)

Here are some important dates in the Metallica timeline between 1981 and 1989.

(NOTE: Not all exact dates have been specified but where possible exact timings have been given.)

1981

June – Ron McGovney formed Leather Charm with James Hetfield.

October – Metallica was officially formed.

1982

March 14 – Metallica played their first ever gig at Radio City in Anaheim, California featuring the recently recruited bassist Ron McGovney.

March 14 – *Ron McGovney's '82 Garage Demo* was recorded.

March 27 – Metallica opened for Saxon at the Whisky A-Go-Go in LA. It was the band's second gig.

April – *Power Metal* demo was recorded.

May 25 – Metallica played a gig at Backbay High School in Costa Mesa.

June 5 – Metallica returned to Radio City in Anaheim for a gig.

June 14 – *Metal Massacre* was released in the USA.

July 3 – Metallica played a gig at the Concert Factory in Costa Mesa.

July 5 – Metallica played a gig at Hollywood's The Troubadour.

July 15 – Metallica played their first party performance at Huntington Beach.

July – *No Life 'Til Leather* demo was released in the USA.

August 2 – Metallica returned to play a gig at Hollywood's The Troubadour.

August 4 – Metallica played a gig at the Whisky A-Go-Go with Steeler and Sound Barrier.

August 18 – Metallica returned to play a gig at Hollywood's The Troubadour with Ratt. They played their first encore.

August 27 – Metallica returned to the Whisky A-Go-Go in LA.

August 29 – Metallica played at HJ's in Hollywood.

September 18 – Metallica played a gig at The Stone in San Francisco; their first gig in the Bay Area.

November 29 – *Metal Up Your Ass Live* demo was recorded at The Old Waldorf in San Francisco.

December 12 – Ron McGovney parted ways with Metallica.

1983

5 March – Metallica played their first gig with Cliff Burton at The Stone.

16 March – *Megaforce* demo was recorded, the last to feature Dave Mustaine, the first to feature Cliff Burton.

11 April – Reportedly to be the day when Dave Mustaine was asked to leave the band.

16 April – Metallica's first live gig (The Showplace in Drover, New Jersey) with new lead guitarist Kirk Hammett.

May 10 – Metallica began recording *Kill 'Em All* at Music America Studios in New York.

May 27 – Metallica finished recording *Kill 'Em All.*

June 25 – *Kill 'Em All* was released in the USA.

July – *Kill 'Em All* was released in the UK.

July 27 – Metallica began the '*Kill 'Em All* For One Tour' with Raven.

August 8 – 'Whiplash' was released as a single in the USA.

September 3 – Metallica finished the '*Kill 'Em All* For One Tour' with Raven at The Stone in San Francisco.

October 24 – *Ride The Lightning* demo was released in the USA.

1984

January 20 – 'Jump In The Fire' was released as a single in the USA.

February 3 – Metallica begin the 'Seven Dates Of Hell Tour', supporting Venom.

February 20 – Metallica began recording *Ride The Lightning* at Sweet Silence Studios in Copenhagen, Denmark.

March 14 – Metallica finished recording *Ride The Lightning*.

March 27 – Metallica played their first UK gig at the London Marquee.

July 16 – 'Seek & Destroy' was released as a single in the USA.

July 27 – *Ride The Lightning* was released in the USA (also released in July in the UK).

August 29 – The 'Seven Dates Of Hell Tour' ended.

November 16 – Metallica commenced the 'Bang That Head That Doesn't Bang Tour'.

November 23 – 'Creeping Death' was released as a single in the USA.

December 20 – The 'Bang That Head That Doesn't Bang Tour' ended.

1985

January 9 – '*Ride The Lightning* Tour' commenced.

March 6 – Bassist James Newsted reportedly attended Metallica's gig in Phoenix, Arizona.

July 15 – *Master Of Puppets* demos were recorded.

August 17 – Metallica performed at the Monsters Of Rock Festival at Castle Donington, England.

August 31 – 'For Whom The Bell Tolls' was released as a single in the USA.

August 31 – Metallica performed at the Day At The Green Festival in Oakland, California.

September 1 – Metallica began recording *Master Of Puppets* at Sweet Silence Studios in Copenhagen, Denmark.

December 26 – Metallica finished recording *Master Of Puppets*.

December 31 – '*Ride The Lightning* Tour' ended.

1986

January 31 – Party band the Spastic Children with James Hetfield on drums played a gig at Ruthie's in San Francisco.

February 20 – Spastic Children played a gig at The Rock in San Francisco.

March 3 – *Master Of Puppets* was released in the USA (also released in March in the UK).

March 27 – 'Damage, Inc. Tour' commenced.

July 2 – 'Master Of Puppets' was released as a single in the USA.

August 1 – 'Battery' was released as a single in the USA.

September 26 – Cliff Burton's final appearance with the band was a gig at the Solnahallen Arena in Stockholm, Sweden.

September 27 – Cliff Burton was killed in a road accident in Sweden in the early hours of the morning.

October 23 – 'Welcome Home (Sanitarium)' was released as a single in the USA.

1987

February 13 – 'Damage, Inc. Tour' ended.

August – Metallica released *The $5.98 EP: Garage Days Revisited.*

August 20 – Metallica toured Europe as part of the 'Monsters Of Rock Festival Tour'.

August 22 – Metallica performed at the Monsters Of Rock Festival at Castle Donington, England.

August 30 – 'The Monsters Of Rock Festival Tour' of Europe ended.

1988

January 28 – Metallica began recording *...And Justice For All* at One On One Recording Studios in LA, California.

May 1 – Metallica finished recording *...And Justice For All.*

May 27 – Metallica toured the United States as part of the 'Monsters Of Rock Festival Tour'.

July 30 – The 'Monsters Of Rock Festival Tour' of the United States ended.

August 25 – *...And Justice For All* was released in the USA.

August 28 – 'Harvester Of Sorrow' released as a single in the USA.

September 6 – '...And Justice For All' was released as a single in the USA.

September 11 – 'Damaged Justice Tour' commenced.

October – *...And Justice For All* was released in the UK and USA.

October 30 – 'Eye Of The Beholder' was released as a single in the USA.

1989

January 10 – 'One' was released as a single in the USA.

October 8 – 'Damaged Justice Tour' ended.

METALLICA'S HEROES ©photos courtesy of Andy Brailsford

Saxon frontman Biff Byford, one of Metallica's NWOBHM heroes and a true metal veteran.

Deep Purple's Ian Gillan. Attending a Purple gig changed Lars Ulrich's life forever.

Motörhead's legendary frontman Lemmy; Metallica's close personal friend and a primary influence on the band and the late bassist Cliff Burton.

Judas Priest's axe-shredding K.K. Downing with the Metal God, Rob Halford.

ACKNOWLEDGEMENTS

The author would like to express his gratitude to the following people who were kindly interviewed for this book: Bailey Brothers, Biff Byford, Jon Collins, Jess Cox, Bernard Doe, Mike Exley, Bill Hale, David Konow, Joel McIver, Bob Nalbandian, Martin Popoff, Ron Quintana, Brian Rademacher, John Ricci, Brian Ross, Xavier Russell, Brian Slagel, Brian Tatler, Ron 'Bumblefoot' Thal, John Tucker, Michael Wagener and Jeff Waters.

Thanks to the following rockers for making this book (and my others) possible and for their ongoing support: Phil and Sue Ashcroft, Andy Brailsford, Bailey Brothers, Jerry Bloom, Dante Bonutto, Ian Christe, Jess Cox, Bernard Doe, Malcolm Dome, John Doran, Mark Eglinton, Mike Exley, Bill Hale, Matthew Hamilton, Mark Hoaksey, Steve Huey, Scott Ian, David Konow, Borivoj Krgin, Dom Lawson, Dave Lewis, Dave Ling, Matthias Mader, Joe Matera, Joel McIver, Bruce Mee, Mick Middles, Bob Nalbandian, Derek Oliver, Dead Pedley, Martin Popoff, James Powell, Greg Prato, Greg Pratt, Ron Quintana, Brian Rademacher, John Ricci, Jason Ritchie, Martin Roach and Independent Music Press, Steven Rosen, Brian Ross, Xavier Russell, Red Shaw, Joe Shooman, Brian Slagel, Brian Tatler, Ron 'Bumblefoot' Thal, Dave Thompson, Kimmo Toivonen, John Tucker, Jaan Uhelszki, Michael Wagener, Mick Wall, Jeff Waters, Joshua Wood and Jeb Wright. Apologies for those names that I'm bound to have forgotten. Also thanks to my parents, Ann and Andrew, my family and good friends, Scott, Rob, Ste, Dave and Graeme.

Finally, special thanks to James Powell, Bernard Doe and Ron Quintana for digging deep into their archives and offering parts of their collections for use in this book.

Visit *www.neildaniels.com*.

BIBLIOGRAPHY & SOURCES

The following publications and websites were integral in making this book possible…

Special thanks to Pat O' Connor at Shockwaves *and Bernard Doe for delving into his* Metal Forces *archive and for letting me quote his interviews extensively; also special thanks to Borivoj Krgin. Check out www.metalforcesmagazine.com. Also www.metallicaworld.co.uk has a nifty archive of previously published interviews that proved very useful for this book. Special thanks to Metallica and Cliff Burton biographer Joel McIver too. A big shout out to them all!*

REFERENCE BOOKS

Betts, Graham. *Complete UK Hit Singles 1952-2005.* (London: Collins, 2005.)

Betts, Graham. *Complete UK Hit Albums: 1956-2005.* (London: Collins, 2005.)

Larkin, Colin. *The Virgin Encyclopaedia Of Rock.* (London: Virgin Books, 1999.)

Roberts, David (Ed.) *British Hit Singles & Albums. (19th Edition)* (London: Guinness World Records Ltd, 2006.)

Strong, Martin C. *The Great Rock Discography. (6th Edition)* (London: Canongate, 2002.)

MUSIC BOOKS

Byford, Biff & Tucker, John. *Never Surrender (Or Nearly Good Looking.)* (Germany: Iron Pages, 2002.)

METALLICA

Christe, Ian. *Sound Of The Beast: The Complete Headbanging History Of Heavy Metal.* (London: Allison & Busby Limited, 2004.)

Konow, David. *Bang Your Head: The Rise And Fall Of Heavy Metal.* (London: Plexus, 2004.)

MacMillan, Malc. *The New Wave Of British Heavy Metal Encyclopaedia.* (Germany: Iron Pages, 2001.)

McIver, Joel. *The Bloody Reign Of Slayer.* (London: Omnibus Press, 2008.)

Mustaine, Dave. *A Life In Metal.* (USA: HarperCollins, 2010.)

Popoff, Martin. *The Collector's Guide To Heavy Metal – Volume 2: The Eighties.* (Canada: Collector's Guide Publishing, 2005.)

Sharpe-Young, Gary. *Thrash Metal.* (London: Zonda Books, 2007.)

Tatler, Brian & Tucker, John. *Am I Evil? The Music, The Myths And Metallica.* (Self-Published: http://www.diamond-head.net, 2010.)

Tucker, John. *Suzie Smiled... The New Wave Of British Heavy Metal.* (Independent Music Press, 2006.)

BOOKS ON METALLICA

Berlinger, Joe & Milner, Greg. *Metallica: This Monster Lives.* (USA: Griffin Trade Paperbacks, 2005.)

Chirazi, Steffan. *So What!: The Good, The Mad And The Ugly.* (USA: Broadway Books, 2004.)

Crocker, Chris. *Metallica: The Frayed Ends Of Metal.* (London: Boxtree, 1995.)

Dome, Malcolm & Ewing, Jerry. *The Encyclopaedia Metallica.* (Surrey: Chrome Dreams, 2007.)

Eglinton, Mark. *James Hetfield: The Wolf At Metallica's Door.* (Independent Music Press, 2010.)

Hadland, Sam. *Metallica: Fuel & Fire – The Illustrated Collector's Guide.* (Canada, Collector's Guide Publishing, 2004.)

Hale, Bill. *Metallica: The Club Daze.* (Canada, ECW Press, 2099.)

Halfin, Ross. *Ultimate Metallica.* (USA: Chronicle, 2010.)

Hotten, Jon. *Metallica.* (London: Music Book Services, 1994.)

Ingham, Cliff. *Metallica: The Stories Behind The Biggest Songs.* (London: Carlton, 2009.)

Irwin, William. *Metallica And Philosophy.* (USA: Wiley-Blackwell, 2007.)

McIver, Joel. *Metallica: And Justice For All.* (London: Omnibus Press, 2009) (3rd Ed)

McIver, Joel. *To Live Is To Die: The Life And Death Of Metallica's Cliff Burton.* (London: Jawbone, 2009.)

Putterford, Mark & Heatley, Michael. *Metallica: In Their Own Words.* (London: Omnibus Press, 1994.)

Stenning, Paul. *Metallica: All That Matters.* (London: Plexus, 2010.)

Wall, Mick & Dome, Malcolm. *Metallica: The Complete Guide To Their Music.* (London: Omnibus Press, 2005.) (2nd Ed)

Wall, Mick. *Enter Night.* (London: Orion, 2010)

MAGAZINES

Artist Magazine / Bass Player / Billboard / BW&BK / Classic Rock / Fireworks / Guitar Magazine / Guitar World Magazine / Guitarist / Hard Rock / Hard Roxx / Headbanger / Hit Parader / Kerrang! / Kerrang! Mega Metal / Melt Down / Metal Edge / Metal Forces / Metal Hammer / Metal Maniacs / MetalXtreme Magazine / Modern Drummer / Modern Guitars / Modern Recording / Musician / NME / Powerplay / RAW / Record Collector / Revolver / Rock Hard / Rock Magazine! / Rolling Stone / Soundcheck! / Sounds / Terrorizer / Thrasher Magazine / Whiplash / Zero Tolerance

WEBSITES

www.metalforcesmagazine.com
http://blogcritics.org/music
http://earcandy_mag.tripod.com/
http://heavymetal.about.com
http://jam.canoe.ca
http://metallicablogmagnetic.com
http://music.msn.com
http://thequietus.com
uk.music.ign.com
www.about.com
www.allmusic.com
www.angelfire.com/rock2/rockinterviews
www.aquarian.com
www.battlehelm.com
www.blasting-zone.com
www.blistering.com
www.bookofhours.net
www.bravewords.com
www.classicrockmagazine.com
www.dailytelegraph.co.uk
www.encyment.com
www.exclaim.ca
www.ew.com

www.fanpop.com
www.getreadytorock.com
www.getreadytoroll.com
www.gibsonguitar.in
www.guardian.co.uk
www.guitar.com
www.guitarcenter.com
www.hardradio.com
www.hellhound.ca
www.ilikethat.com
www.junkonline.net
www.kaos2000.net
www.latimes.com
www.metal-archives.com
www.metalhammer.co.uk
www.metal-observer.com
www.metal-rules.com
www.metalstorm.net
www.metalsucks.com
www.metalunderground.com
www.mixonline.com
www.moshville.com
www.musicradar.com
www.musicrooms.net
www.noisecreep.com
www.punknews.org
www.thequietus.com
www.review-mag.com
http://robertchristgau.com/get_artist.php
www.rocksbackpages.com
www.rockzone.com
www.shockwave.com
www.sputnikmusic.com
www.storyofthestars.com
www.stylusmagazine.com
www.suite101.com
www.sundaysun.co.uk

METALLICA

www.thrashhits.com
www.triplem.com
www.ultimate-guitar.com
www.virginmega.com

WEBSITES ON METALLICA

www.metallica.com
www.loureedmetallica.com
www.myspace.com/metallica
www.facebook.com/Metallica
www.encycmet.com
www.metallicaworld.co.uk
www.allmetallica.com
www.metallicabb.com
www.1metallica.s5.com
www.metallifukinca.com
metallicablogmagnetic.com

END NOTES

[i] Kirk Hammett quote; interviewer unknown, *Kirkus Maximus* ('The Expanding World Of Kirk Hammett,') 1996.

[ii] Lars Ulrich quote; Bernard Doe interview, *Metal Forces*, 1984.

[iii] Lars Ulrich quote; interviewer unknown, 'Married To Metal,' 1995.

[iv] Lars Ulrich quote; interviewer unknown, *Revolver*, 2011.

[v] Brian Tatler quote; author interview, 2011.

[vi] Brian Tatler quote; author interview, 2011.

[vii] Bob Nalbandian quote; author interview, 2011.

[viii] Bob Nalbandian quote; author interview, 2011.

[ix] James Hetfield quote; interviewer unknown, *Virginmega.com*, 1999.

[x] Ron McGovney quote; Pat O'Connor interview, *Shockwaves*, 1997.

[xi] James Hetfield quote; interviewer unknown, *Kerrang! Legends: Metallica.*

[xii] James Hetfield quote; interviewer unknown, *Guitar World Magazine*, 1998.

[xiii] Brian Slagel quote; author interview, 2011.

[xiv] Brian Slagel quote; author interview, 2011.

[xv] Ron Quintana quote; author interview, 2011.

[xvi] Ron Quintana quote; author interview, 2011.

[xvii] Ron Quintana quote; author interview, 2011.

[xviii] Brian Tatler quote; author interview, *Fireworks*, 2009.

[xix] Ron Quintana quote; author interview, 2011.

[xx] Dave Mustaine quote; PD Freeman interview, *MSN Music*, 2011.

[xxi] Dave Mustaine quote; Robert Pally interview, *Ear Candy*, 2002.

[xxii] Bob Nalbandian quote; author interview, 2011.

[xxiii] Ron McGovney quote; Pat O'Connor interview, *Shockwaves*, 1997.

[xxiv] James Hetfield quote; interviewer unknown, *Kerrang! Legends: Metallica.*

[xxv] Ron McGovney quote; Pat O'Connor interview, *Shockwaves*, 1997.

[xxvi] Lars Ulrich quote; Bernard Doe interview, *Metal Forces*, 1984.

[xxvii] Lars Ulrich quote; Bernard Doe interview, *Metal Forces*, 1984.

[xxviii] Lloyd Grant quote; Bob Nalbandian interview, *Shockwaves*, 1997.

[xxix] Lloyd Grant quote; Bob Nalbandian interview, *Shockwaves*, 1997.

[xxx] Bill Hale quote; author interview, 2011.

[xxxi] Brian Ross quote; author interview, 2011.

[xxxii] Bernard Doe quote; author interview, 2011.

[xxxiii] Ron McGovney quote; Pat O'Connor interview, *Shockwaves*, 1997.

[xxxiv] Xavier Russell quote; author interview, 2009.

[xxxv] Xavier Russell quote; author interview, 2009.

[xxxvi] Brian Slagel quote; author interview, 2011.

[xxxvii] James Hetfield quote; interviewer unknown, *Metal Hammer*, 1999.

[xxxviii] Ron McGovney quote; Pat O'Connor interview, *Shockwaves*, 1997.

[xxxix] Ron McGovney quote; Pat O'Connor interview, *Shockwaves*, 1997.

[xl] Cliff Burton quote; interviewer unknown, February, 1986. *(Referenced on www.metallicaworld.co.uk.)*

[xli] Brian Slagel quote; author interview, 2011.

[xlii] Bill Hale quote; author interview, 2011.

[xliii] Jan Burton quote; Harald O. interview, year and publication unknown. *(Referenced on www.metallicaworld.co.uk.)*

[xliv] Joel McIver quote; author interview, 2011.

[xlv] Biff Byford quote; author interview, *Fireworks*, 2008.

[xlvi] Brian Slagel quote; author interview, 2009.

[xlvii] Bob Nalbandian quote; author interview, 2011.

[xlviii] Lars Ulrich quote; Bernard Doe interview, *Metal Forces*, 1984.

[xlix] James Hetfield quote; Greg Pratt interview, *Bravewords.com*, 2008.

[l] Bob Nalbandian quote; author interview, 2011.

[li] Joel McIver quote; author interview, 2011.

[lii] Lars Ulrich quote; Bernard Doe interview, *Metal Forces*, 1984.

[liii] Lars Ulrich quote; Bernard Doe interview, *Metal Forces*, 1984.

[liv] Lars Ulrich quote; interviewer unknown, *Kerrang! Legends: Metallica*.

[lv] Lars Ulrich quote; Bernard Doe interview, *Metal Forces*, 1984.

[lvi] Lars Ulrich quote; interviewer unknown, *Guitar World*, 1991.

[lvii] Ron Quintana quote; author interview, 2011.

[lviii] Bill Hale quote; author interview, 2011.

[lix] Kirk Hammett quote; Jaan Uhelszki interview, *Musicradar.com*, 2008.

[lx] Kirk Hammett quote; Douglas J Noble, *Guitar Magazine*, 'Load Era 1,' 1996. *(Referenced on www.metallicaworld.co.uk.)*

[lxi] Kirk Hammett quote; Ryan Cooper interview, *About.com/Punk Music*, 2009.

[lxii] Kirk Hammett quote; Jaan Uhelszki interview, *Musicradar.com*, 2008.

[lxiii] Dave Mustaine quote; Bob Nalbandian interview, *Shockwaves*, 1984.

[lxiv] Lars Ulrich quote; interviewer unknown, *Guitarcenter.com*, 2001.

[lxv] Bill Hale quote; author interview, 2011.

[lxvi] Kirk Hammett quote; interviewer unknown, *Rolling Stone* , 'Pretty Hate Machine,' 1996.

[lxvii] Brian Slagel quote; author interview, 2011.

[lxviii] James Hetfield quote; interviewer unknown, *Guitar World Magazine*, 1998.

[lxix] Lars Ulrich quote; Bernard Doe interview, *Metal Forces*, 1984.

[lxx] Kirk Hammett quote; Jaan Uhelszki interview, *Musicradar.com*, 2008.

[lxxi] Kirk Hammett quote; Jaan Uhelszki interview, *Musicradar.com*, 2008.

[lxxii] Kirk Hammett quote; Therese Owen interview, *Tonight* newspaper, year unknown.

[lxxiii] Bernard Doe quote; author interview, 2011.

[lxxiv] Kirk Hammett quote; interviewer unknown, *Rolling Stone* , 'Pretty Hate Machine,' 1996.

[lxxv] Bernard Doe quote; author interview, 2010.

[lxxvi] Martin Popoff quote; author interview, 2011.

[lxxvii] Brian Tatler quote; author interview, 2011.

[lxxviii] Brian Tatler quote; author interview, 2011.

[lxxix] Dave Grohl quote; interviewer unknown, *Kerrang!*, 2007.

[lxxx] Scott Ian quote; Jon Wiederhorn interview, *Noisecreep*, year unknown.

[lxxxi] James Hetfield quote; interviewer unknown, *Metal Hammer*, 1999.

[lxxxii] James Hetfield quote; interviewer unknown, *Metal Hammer*, 1999.

[lxxxiii] James Hetfield quote; interviewer unknown, *Guitar World Magazine*, 1998.

[lxxxiv] Cliff Burton quote; interviewer unknown, February, 1986. *(Referenced on www.metallicaworld.co.uk.)*

[lxxxv] James Hetfield quote; interviewer unknown, 'Write The Lightning,' 1996.

[lxxxvi] James Hetfield quote; interviewer unknown, 'Write The Lightning,' 1996.

[lxxxvii] James Hetfield quote; interviewer unknown, *Guitar World Magazine*, 1998.

[lxxxviii] Kirk Hammett quote; Pushead interview, *Thrasher Magazine*, 1986.

[lxxxix] Jeff Waters quote; author interview, 2006.

[xc] John Ricci quote; author interview, 2011.

[xci] David Konow quote; author interview, 2011.

[xcii] Brian Slagel quote; author interview, 2011.

[xciii] Jon Collins quote; author interview, 2011.

[xciv] Martin Popoff quote; author interview, 2011.

[xcv] Lars Ulrich quote; interviewer unknown 'Married To Metal,' 1995.

[xcvi] Kirk Hammett quote; interviewer unknown, *Guitar World Magazine*, 1998.

[xcvii] James Hetfield quote; Douglas J Noble, *Guitar Magazine*, 'Load Era 1,' 1996. *(Referenced on www.metallicaworld.co.uk.)*

[xcviii] Lars Ulrich quote; Bernard Doe interview, *Metal Forces*, 1984.

[xcix] Kirk Hammett quote; Jaan Uhelszki interview, *Musicradar.com*, 2008.

[c] Mike Exley quote; author interview, 2011.

[ci] Jess Cox quote; author interview, 2011.

[cii] John Ricci quote; author interview, 2011.

[ciii] James Hetfield quote; interviewer unknown, *Guitar World Magazine*, 1998.

[civ] Brian Slagel quote; author interview, 2011.

[cv] Bernard Doe quote; author interview, 2011.

[cvi] Lars Ulrich quote; Bernard Doe interview, *Metal Forces*, 1984.

[cvii] Martin Popoff quote; author interview, 2011.

[cviii] James Hetfield quote; Douglas J Noble, *Guitar Magazine*, 'Load Era 1,' 1996. *(Referenced on www.metallicaworld.co.uk.)*

[cix] Lars Ulrich quote; Bernard Doe interview, *Metal Forces*, 1984.

[cx] Brian Ross quote; author interview, 2011.

[cxi] James Hetfield quote; interviewer unknown, *Virginmega.com*, 1999.

[cxii] Bernard Doe quote; author interview, 2011.

[cxiii] Bernard Doe quote; author interview, 2011.

[cxiv] James Hetfield quote; interviewer unknown, *Guitar Magazine*, 1991.

[cxv] Jeff Waters quote; author interview, 2006.

[cxvi] Scott Ian quote; interviewer unknown, *Metal Hammer* (quote supplied by Scott Ian to the author, 2011.)

[cxvii] James Newsted quote; interviewer unknown, *Kerrang!*, 1986.

[cxviii] Jeff Waters quote; author interview, 2006.

[cxix] Lars Ulrich quote; Bernard Doe interview, *Metal Forces*, 1984.

[cxx] Lars Ulrich quote; Bernard Doe interview, *Metal Forces*, 1986.

[cxxi] Cliff Burton quote; interviewer unknown, February, 1986. *(Referenced on www.metallicaworld.co.uk.)*

[cxxii] Kirk Hammett quote; interviewer unknown, *Guitar World Magazine*, 1998.

[cxxiii] James Hetfield quote; interviewer unknown, *Rolling Stone* , 'Pretty Hate Machine,' 1996.

[cxxiv] Michael Wagener quote; author interview, 2011.

[cxxv] Lars Ulrich quote; Bernard Doe interview, *Metal Forces*, 1986.

[cxxvi] Kirk Hammett quote; Pushead interview, *Thrasher Magazine*, 1986.

[cxxvii] James Hetfield quote; Pushead interview, *Thrasher Magazine*, 1986.

[cxxviii] James Hetfield quote; Douglas J Noble, *Guitar Magazine*, 'Load Era 1,' 1996. *(Referenced on www.metallicaworld.co.uk.)*

[cxxix] Lars Ulrich quote; Richard Gehr interview, *Music & Sound Output*, archived at Rock's Backpages, 1988.

[cxxx] Joel McIver quote, author interview, 2011.

[cxxxi] Lars Ulrich quote; Bernard Doe interview, *Metal Forces*, 1986.

[cxxxii] Bernard Doe quote; author interview, 2011.

cxxxiii Martin Popoff quote; author interview, 2011.

cxxxiv Matt Harvey quote; Justin M, Norton interview, *Hellhound.ca,* 2011.

cxxxv Lars Ulrich quote; Bernard Doe interview, *Metal Forces*, 1990.

cxxxvi Kirk Hammett quote; Pushead interview, *Thrasher Magazine*, 1986.

cxxxvii Kirk Hammett quote; Pushead interview, *Thrasher Magazine*, 1986.

cxxxviii James Hetfield quote; interviewer unknown, *Metal Hammer*, 1999.

cxxxix Xavier Russell quote; author interview, 2009.

cxl James Hetfield quote; interviewer unknown, 'Load Perspectives,' 1996. *(Referenced on www.metallicaworld.co.uk.)*

cxli Brian Tatler quote; author interview, 2011.

cxlii James Hetfield quote; interviewer unknown, *Dagens Nyheter*, 2006.

cxliii Brian Slagel quote; author interview, 2011.

cxliv Bill Hale quote; author interview, 2011.

cxlv Bill Hale quote; author interview, 2011.

cxlvi Lars Ulrich quote; interviewer unknown, *Kerrang! Legends: Metallica.*

cxlvii James Newsted quote; interviewee unknown, *Metal Rules*, 2003.

cxlviii James Newsted quote; Chris Harris interview, *Rolling Stone*, 2009.

cxlix James Newsted quote; interviewer unknown, 1989. *(Referenced on www.metallicaworld.co.uk.)*

cl James Hetfield quote; interviewer unknown, 1991. *(Referenced on www.metallicaworld.co.uk.)*

cli Kirk Hammett, quote; interviewer unknown, 'Load Perspectives,' 1996.

clii Lars Ulrich quote; Bernard Doe interview, *Metal Forces*, 1989.

cliii Pushead quote; interviewee unknown, *Transworld Skateboarding*, 2002.

cliv Kirk Hammett quote; interviewer unknown, *Guitar World Magazine*, 1998.

clv Lars Ulrich quote; interviewer unknown, 'Garage Days,' 1998. *(Referenced on www.metallicaworld.co.uk.)*

clvi Lars Ulrich quote; interviewer unknown, 'Garage Days,' 1998. *(Referenced on www.metallicaworld.co.uk.)*

clvii Kirk Hammett quote; interviewer unknown, *Guitar World Magazine*, 1998.

clviii Dez Bailey quote; author interview, 2011.

clix Lars Ulrich quote; Richard Gehr interview, *Music & Sound Output,* archived at *Rock's Backpages*, 1988.

clx James Newsted quote; Joel McIver interview, author of *To Live Is To Die: The Life And Death Of Metallica's Cliff Burton.*

clxi James Newsted quote; interviewer unknown, 1989. *(Referenced on www.metallicaworld.co.uk.)*

clxii Lars Ulrich and James Hetfield quote; Richard Gehr interview, *Music & Sound Output,* archived at *Rock's Backpages*, 1988.

clxiii Lars Ulrich quote; Borivoj Krgin interview, *Metal Forces*, 1988.

clxiv Kirk Hammett; quote; interviewer unknown, *Rolling Stone* , 'Pretty Hate Machine,' 1996.

clxv James Newsted quote; Joel McIver interview, author of *To Live Is To Die: The Life And Death*

Of Metallica's Cliff Burton.

clxvi James Newsted quote; Joel McIver interview, author of *To Live Is To Die: The Life And Death Of Metallica's Cliff Burton.*

clxvii James Hetfield quote; Douglas J Noble interview, *Guitar Magazine*, 1996.

clxviii Lars Ulrich quote; Borivoj Krgin interview, *Metal Forces*, 1988.

clxix Kirk Hammett quote; interviewer unknown, *Guitar.com*, 1999.

clxx James Hetfield quote; interviewer unknown, *Dagens Nyheter*, 2006.

clxxi Joel McIver quote; author interview, 2011.

clxxii Bob Nalbandian quote; author interview, 2011.

clxxiii James Hetfield quote; interviewer unknown, *Guitar World Magazine*, 1998.

clxxiv James Newsted quote; interviewer unknown, *Bass Player*, 1996.

clxxv James Hetfield quote; Pushead interview, *Thrasher Magazine*, 1986.

clxxvi James Hetfield quote; interviewer unknown, *Rolling Stone* , 'Pretty Hate Machine,' 1996.

clxxvii Lars Ulrich quote; Borivoj Krgin interview, *Metal Forces*, 1988.

clxxviii James Newsted quote; Al Gomes and A. Michelle, *The Nice Paper*, 1992.

clxxix James Newsted quote; Vince Levalois interview, *MetalXtreme*, 2003.

clxxx Lars Ulrich quote; Bernard Doe interview, *Metal Forces*, 1986.

clxxxi Brian Rademacher quote; author interview, 2011.

clxxxii James Hetfield quote; interviewer unknown, *Metal Hammer*, 1999.

clxxxiii James Newsted quote; Martin Carlsson interview, *Expressen*, 2002.

clxxxiv Lars Ulrich quote; Borivoj Krgin interview, *Metal Forces*, 1988.

clxxxv James Newsted quote; Joel McIver interview, author of *To Live Is To Die: The Life And Death Of Metallica's Cliff Burton.*

clxxxvi James Hetfield quote; Richard Gehr interview, *Music & Sound Output*, archived at *Rock's Backpages*, 1988.

clxxxvii James Hetfield quote; Richard Gehr interview, *Music & Sound Output*, archived at *Rock's Backpages*, 1988.

clxxxviii Lars Ulrich quote; Borivoj Krgin interview, *Metal Forces*, 1988.

clxxxix Joel McIver quote; author interview, 2011.

cxc Bob Nalbandian quote; author interview, 2011.

cxci Bob Nalbandian quote; author interview, 2011.

cxcii James Newsted quote; Axl Rosenburg interview, *Metalsucks*, 2010.

cxciii Kirk Hammett quote; interviewer unknown, *Guitar World Magazine*, 1998.

cxciv Lars Ulrich quote; Borivoj Krgin interview, *Metal Forces*, 1988.

cxcv Bernard Doe quote; author interview, 2011.

cxcvi Bill Hale quote; author interview, 2011.

cxcvii Martin Popoff quote; author interview, 2011.

[cxcviii] Lars Ulrich quote; Bernard Doe interview, *Metal Forces*, 1990.

[cxcix] James Hetfield quote; Douglas J Noble, *Guitar Magazine*, 'Load Era I,' 1996. *(Referenced on www.metallicaworld.co.uk.)*

[cc] James Hetfield quote; interviewer unknown, *Virginmega.com*, 1999.

[cci] John Ricci quote; author interview, 2011.

[ccii] Lars Ulrich quote; interviewer unknown 'Married To Metal,' 1995.

[cciii] James Newsted quote; Al Gomes and A. Michelle, *The Nice Paper*, 1992.

[cciv] Lars Ulrich quote; interviewer unknown, 'Summer Sanitarium,' 2000.

[ccv] Lars Ulrich quote; Bernard Doe interview, *Metal Forces*, 1990.

[ccvi] James Newsted quote; interviewer unknown, 1989. *(Referenced on www.metallicaworld.co.uk.)*

[ccvii] Lars Ulrich quote; Bernard Doe interview, *Metal Forces*, 1989.

[ccviii] James Newsted quote; Al Gomes and A. Michelle, *The Nice Paper*, 1992.

[ccix] Lars Ulrich quote; Bernard Doe interview, *Metal Forces*, 1989.

[ccx] Lars Ulrich quote; interviewer unknown, *Rolling Stone*, 1999.

[ccxi] James Hetfield quote; interviewer unknown, *Triplem.com*, 2010.

[ccxii] Kirk Hammett quote; Shawn Fernandes interview, *Gibson Guitar*, 2011.

[ccxiii] Lars Ulrich quote; Bernard Doe interview, *Metal Forces*, 1989.

[ccxiv] James Newsted quote; Al Gomes and A. Michelle, *The Nice Paper*, 1992.

[ccxv] Brian Tatler quote; author interview, 2011.

ccxvi James Hetfield quote; interviewer unknown, *Guitar World Magazine*, 1998.

ccxvii Lars Ulrich quote; Borivoj Krgin interview, *Metal Forces*, 1988.

ccxviii Kirk Hammett quote; interviewer unknown, *Rolling Stone* , 'Pretty Hate Machine,' 1996.

ccxix Lars Ulrich quote; interviewer unknown, *Guitarcenter.com*, 2001.

ccxx James Newsted quote; interviewer unknown, *Metal Edge*, 1997.

ccxxi Kirk Hammett quote; Shawn Fernandes interview, *Gibson Guitar*, 2011.

ccxxii James Newsted quote; Martin Carlsson interview, *Expressen*, 2002.

ccxxiii Xavier Russell quote; author interview, 2011.

ccxxiv John Ricci quote; author interview, 2011.

ccxxv Bob Nalbandian quote; author interview, 2011.

ccxxvi James Newsted quote; Al Gomes and A. Michelle, *The Nice Paper*, 1992.

ccxxvii Brian Slagel quote; author interview, 2011.

ccxxviii Bill Hale quote; author interview, 2011.

ccxxix Bob Nalbandian quote; author interview, 2011.

ccxxx John Ricci quote; author interview, 2011.

ccxxxi Lars Ulrich quote; interviewer unknown 'Married To Metal,' 1995.

ccxxxi Lars Ulrich quote; interviewer unknown, 1991. (Referenced on *www.metallicaworld.co.uk.*)

ccxxxiii Bob Nalbandian quote; author interview, 2011.

ccxxxiv Joel McIver quote; author interview, 2011.

ccxxxv Xavier Russell quote; author interview, 2011.

ccxxxvi Bob Nalbandian quote; author interview, 2011.

ccxxxvii James Hetfield quote; Greg Pratt interview, *Bravewords.com*, 2008.

ccxxxviii Lars Ulrich quote; interviewer unknown 'Married To Metal,' 1995.

ccxxxix Bill Hale quote; author interview, 2011.

ccxl Lars Ulrich quote; Bernard Doe interview, *Metal Forces*, 1986.

ccxli Lars Ulrich quote; Bernard Doe interview, *Metal Forces*, 1984.

ALSO ON INDEPENDENT MUSIC PRESS

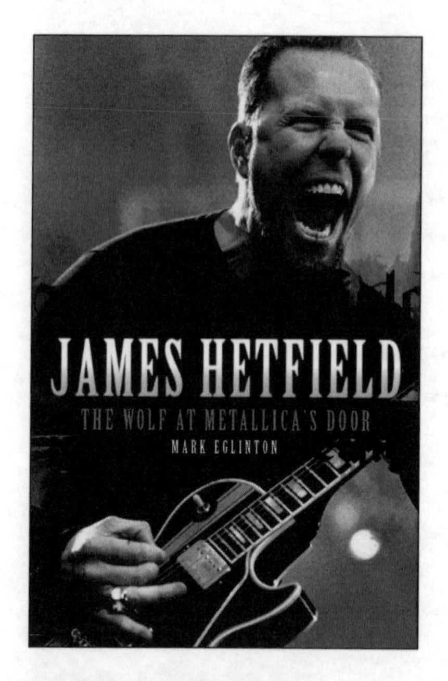

JAMES HETFIELD: THE WOLF AT METALLICA'S DOOR

by Mark Eglinton

The first and only biography of Hetfield, frontman of the biggest rock band of the modern era. Hetfield's overwhelming presence has always guided Metallica's every dramatic step. However, behind the scenes was a complex band fronted by a genius who had his own personal battle to fight – throwing the future of Metallica into considerable doubt. His subsequent re-emergence as a re-invented rock legend is a personal and professional triumph. Author and Metallica expert Mark Eglinton has compiled an exhaustive array of exclusive and first-hand interviews from key players in the story, and in so doing has constructed the definitive biography on Metallica's frontman.

ISBN: 978-1-906191-04-7 Paperback, 208 Pgs including 1x8 pgs b/w pics, 234x153mm World Rights £12.99

ALSO ON INDEPENDENT MUSIC PRESS

THE NEW WAVE OF BRITISH HEAVY METAL

SUZIE SMILED

by John Tucker

This book tells the definitive and complete history of the NWOBHM, from its formation during the late 1970s, through its numerous peaks and troughs in the 1980s and on to its current status as one of rock music's most influential genres. The most famous exponents of this New Wave are stadium-selling acts such as Motörhead, Def Leppard and the currently-enormous-again Iron Maiden, but there are also scores of other acts who have been selling millions of records to the movement's enormous fan-base for years.

Suzie Smiled ... describes what it was like to be writing and playing heavy metal in the post-punk era and sets the music in the bleak social context of the time. This book is the first ever collection of stories from the bands of the NWOBHM. Through a mixture of exclusive new interviews, contemporary articles and unpublished photographs, *Suzie Smiled...* lets the musicians tell the story, including how some of the greatest heavy metal songs ever written were created.

ISBN 978-0-9549704-7-5 256 Pages
234x153mm, Paperback, 1x8 pgs b/w pics, World Rights £12.99